THE MA

MARY SHELLEY'S
FRANKENSTEIN

THE MAKING OF
MARY SHELLEY'S
FRANKENSTEIN

DAISY HAY

Bodleian Library
UNIVERSITY OF OXFORD

First published in 2019 by the Bodleian Library
Broad Street, Oxford OX1 3BG
www.bodleianshop.co.uk

ISBN: 978 1 85124 486 7

Cover design by Dot Little at the Bodleian Library

Designed and typeset by Laura Parker in 9.4 on 16.44 Fedra Serif Pro

Printed and bound in China by C&C Offset Printing Co. Ltd on 157gsm
Chinese Hua Xia Sun matt art paper

British Library Catalogue in Publishing Data

A CIP record of this publication is available from the British Library

CONTENTS

ACKNOWLEDGEMENTS

My thanks go to my agent Clare Alexander, and to Janet Phillips, Leanda Shrimpton, Susie Foster and Samuel Fanous of Bodleian Library Publishing for all they have done to bring this book to fruition. For his invaluable assistance in untangling the manuscripts of *Frankenstein* I am indebted to Bruce Barker-Benfield, and I thank Nora Crook for teaching me how to be a scholar of both Shelleys. I could not have written my account of Mary Shelley's creative process without the pioneering work of the late Charles Robinson, whose presence in the world of Romantic studies will be very much missed. Thank you to Alexandra Harris for more words of creative wisdom than can be counted, and to Amanda Mackenzie Stuart and Matthew Santer for reading drafts and for much else besides. It has been a pleasure and a privilege to teach *Frankenstein* to successive cohorts of students in the Department of English and Film at the University of Exeter and I dedicate this book to them, in gratitude for their enthusiasm, generosity and insight.

PREFACE

Invention, it must be humbly admitted,
does not consist in creating out of void, but out of chaos.[1]

Frankenstein is a novel deeply interested in the subject of creation. Its subtitle is *The Modern Prometheus*, and it reworks the creation myths of Prometheus and Genesis in ways that continue to reverberate down the centuries. In the 200 years since its first publication it has become a metaphor, and the story of its creation a myth in its own right.

The plot of *Frankenstein* is quickly told. Walton the Arctic explorer takes onto his ice-bound ship a stranger who, as he lies dying, relates the extraordinary story of his life. Victor Frankenstein is a young man of good family, who spends a happy youth at his family home outside Geneva. As a student at the University of Ingolstadt he turns away from the realms of institutionalized science to create a Creature from the bodies of the dead, from whom he then flees in horror when it becomes clear that his efforts to animate the Creature with the spark of life have been successful. Left alone in the world the Creature tries to befriend the men and women he meets, but at every turn he is cruelly rejected

1. This recently discovered portrait is inscribed on the reverse 'Mary Shelley / Richard Rothwell R.H.A. 1800–1868'. No authenticated images survive of Mary Shelley as a young woman.

by people who cannot see past his monstrous visage. Rejection makes him cruel in his turn and he takes revenge on his creator by attacking those to whom Frankenstein is closest: first his brother William, then his friend Henry and finally his wife Elizabeth. Creator and Creature have an encounter on the slopes of Mont Blanc, after which Frankenstein reluctantly agrees to honour his parental responsibilities by creating a female companion for his offspring. The Creature pursues him to England and then back to Geneva before finally Frankenstein turns pursuer himself as the novel's central disasters unfold. Once he has related his story Frankenstein dies aboard Walton's ship, leaving Walton himself to face the Creature in the novel's climactic scene. The story ends as the Creature disappears into the mist, leaving Walton gazing in wonder at an empty horizon.

The central facts of *Frankenstein*'s inception – a stormy summer, a brilliant young writer defined by her parentage and relationships with others, an evening of ghost stories – have, like the novel itself, become the stuff of literary legend. How then, does one write about the making of *Frankenstein*? One way might be to imitate Frankenstein the creator, who fashions his Creature through a process of assemblage. He lurks in vaults and charnel houses, purloining body parts in order to animate a new being. 'My attention', he writes, 'was fixed upon every object the most insupportable to the delicacy of the human feelings.'[2] In this book I will take my lead partly from him, charting the story of the novel's birth through an assemblage of objects and images. Many of these images are drawn from the collections of the Bodleian Library, Oxford, where the manuscripts of *Frankenstein* are held.

I will also take my lead from *Frankenstein*'s author, Mary Shelley, who in her Introduction to the 1831 edition of the novel published a narrative of the circumstances in which the work she termed her 'hideous progeny' took flight. She wrote this account when she was thirty-three and already a widow of nine years' standing. She was concerned not with charnel houses or tombs, but with memories of a congenial and productive summer, spent among friends. *Frankenstein*, she recalled, 'was the offspring of happy days, when death and grief were but words, which found no true echo in my heart. Its several pages speak of many a walk, many a drive, and many a conversation, when I was not alone; and my companion was one who, in this world, I shall never see more.' 'This for myself', she continues. 'My readers have nothing to do with these associations.'[3]

Assemblage; conversation; association: these are some of the words that reverberate through the story of the making of *Frankenstein*. The novel was inspired and influenced by the people amongst whom its eighteen-year-old author lived, and by the places and historical dramas that formed the backdrop for her youth. Yet in her 1831 Introduction Mary Shelley also offers a more unsettling account of the imagination as the space where dark materials coalesce into matter. Invention, she writes, 'can give form to dark, shapeless substances, but cannot bring into being the substance itself'. Creation, she insists, is the product not of a void, but of chaos. In this spirit this book will journey into the places, moments and conversations of *Frankenstein*'s creation, in search of its essential, brilliant chaos.

1

TIME

In the early summer of 1816, Mary Shelley arrived on the shores of Lake Geneva. Her name at that point was not in fact Shelley but Mary Wollstonecraft Godwin.[1] She and Percy Bysshe Shelley had eloped two years earlier but were not married, and Shelley was married to somebody else. Their party included their baby William, born in the January of that year, and Mary's stepsister Claire Clairmont, at whose instigation they had travelled to Switzerland. In the spring of 1816 Claire had conducted a brief affair with Lord Byron, the most famous (and infamous) poet of the moment, and she was determined to prolong their dalliance by following him to Geneva.

Byron had tired of Claire by the time he arrived in Switzerland and her efforts to re-attract his attention met with little success. He was much more interested in the presence of Shelley, whose work he knew by reputation. Friendship between the two men flourished, a pattern of daily visits between their households emerged and when storms reverberated around Lake Geneva the group retreated inside to

2. Portrait of Mary Wollstonecraft Shelley by Richard Rothwell, c.1840.

talk and tell stories at Byron's house, the Villa Diodati. One evening Byron proposed that they should all write ghost stories by way of entertainment. In her 1831 account of the Genevan summer Mary claimed that while everyone else rapidly settled down to write she remained at a loss for her tale. '*Have you thought of a story?* I was asked each morning,' she recalled. 'Each morning I was forced to reply with a mortifying negative.'[2]

Mary went on to describe how, a few evenings later, she found herself listening to a conversation between Shelley and Byron about the philosophy of life and the experiments of Erasmus Darwin. 'Night waned upon this talk,' she wrote. 'When I placed my head on my pillow, I did not sleep, nor could I be said to think. My imagination, unbidden, possessed and guided me, gifting the successive images that arose in my mind with a vividness far beyond the usual bounds of reverie. I saw – with shut eyes, but acute mental vision, – I saw the pale student of unhallowed arts kneeling beside the thing he had put together. I saw the hideous phantasm of a man stretched out, and then, on the working of some powerful engine, show signs of life, and stir with an uneasy, half vital motion.' The vision unfolded still further and the following morning Mary was able to report in triumph that she had thought of a story. 'I began that day with the words, *It was on a dreary night in November*, making only a transcript of the grim terrors of my waking dream.'[3]

This account of *Frankenstein*'s genesis has been studied by scholars almost as intensively as the novel itself. Biographers have tallied it

3. Portrait of Percy Bysshe Shelley by Amelia Curran, 1819. This was the only image of Shelley captured in his lifetime.

against entries in the Shelleys' joint diary, noting discrepancies and the way in which conversations that apparently happened over several evenings are elided in Mary's telling. Literary critics have tracked the Introduction's debts to other writers, and other accounts of inspiration. Many have noted the similarity between Mary's 'waking dream' and that described by Coleridge in the Preface to 'Kubla Kahn':

> The author continued for about three hours in a profound sleep, at least of the external senses, during which time he has the most vivid confidence that he could not have composed less than from two to three hundred lines; if that indeed can be called composition in which all the images rose up before him as things, with a parallel production of the correspondent expressions, without any sensation or consciousness of effort.[4]

The points of connection between the two accounts are clear: unbidden images descending to the creative mind, the strong sense of an artistic vision received by a medium fully formed. Both stories contribute to and derive from a conception of creative genius that became very influential in the late eighteenth century, in which the artist is inspired not by a muse but through a process of subconscious internalization of external things until the imagination becomes its own source of vision. This idea had its most famous articulation in Wordsworth's Preface to *Lyrical Ballads*, in which the poet justified his use of vernacular forms by arguing that poetry owed its power to the poet's attuned acknowledgement of the interdependence of nature, emotions and language. His principal object, Wordsworth wrote,

4. Portrait of George Gordon, Lord Byron, by Richard Westall, 1813.

was to take incidents drawn from everyday life, described in everyday language, and 'to throw over them a certain colouring of imagination, whereby ordinary things should be presented to the mind in an unusual way; and, further, and above all, to make these incidents and situations interesting by tracing in them, truly though not ostentatiously, the primary laws of our nature'.[5]

When Mary described invention as originating not out of the void but of chaos, therefore, she was reformulating the ideas of Wordsworth and Coleridge for her own ends. What inspiration, then, did the historical moment of *Frankenstein*'s composition offer her? What ideas were circulating around her? Whose were the voices peopling the chaos of her imagination, and what were they saying? We can start our search for answers once again in her Introduction, by investigating her account of the things she was reading, thinking and talking about in the days and weeks leading up to her 'waking dream'.

A first clue comes early on. 'It proved a wet, ungenial summer, and incessant rain often confined us for days to the house,' Mary wrote. 'Some volumes of ghost stories, translated from the German into French, fell into our hands.'[6] The volume in question was *Fantasmagoriana*, an anthology of stories collected and translated by Jean-Baptiste Eyriès and published in Paris in 1812. Mary's account of the stories suggests she misremembered several of them, but it was less the detail of the plots that inspired her than the experience of reading ghost stories among friends, watching their reactions to tales of monstrousness and gothic melodrama. *Frankenstein* has often been characterized as a fine example of Gothic fiction, and it certainly shares some of the genre's interests and tendencies. But Mary herself was sceptical about the credulousness of the form, as her rather dismissive account of a story written by Byron's travelling companion John Polidori illustrates. 'Poor Polidori', she remembered, 'had some terrible idea about a skull-headed lady, who was so punished for peeping through a key-hole – what to see I forget – something very shocking and wrong of course ... he did not know what to do with her, and was obliged to despatch her to the tomb of the Capulets.'[7] From the outset she aimed to write about more than shocks and spooks, but she was nevertheless interested in the impact the reading of *Fantasmagoriana* had on her companions and on the power of other-worldly horrors to inspire creativity and to generate more unpredictable reactions. She had seen something of this herself two years earlier, during an evening in which Shelley frightened Claire into hysterics by telling her stories, and during the storms of 1816 Mary began to think through the ways in which the literary power of monstrousness might be harnessed.

A still more literal iteration of this power presented itself at the end of another evening at the Villa Diodati, during which Byron recited some verses of Coleridge's *Christabel*. *Christabel* tells the story of a female temptress who invades the stronghold of a medieval castle through seduction and stealth until only the poem's eponymous heroine is aware of her snake-like, enchantress qualities (fig. 5). Polidori, who was a practising doctor, recalled that the reading produced a dramatic reaction in Shelley, who, 'suddenly shrieking and putting his hands to his head, ran of the room with a candle ... He was looking at Mrs S[helley], and suddenly thought of a woman he had heard of who had eyes instead of nipples which, taking hold of his mind, horrified him.'[8] Polidori made Shelley inhale ether to calm down and threw water on his face but for Mary the combustible nature of tales of monstrous creatures and lively imaginations produced visions less easily dismissed.

SO HALF-WAY FROM THE BED SHE ROSE,
AND ON HER ELBOW DID RECLINE
TO LOOK AT THE LADY GERALDINE.

Frankenstein draws on these individual instances and observations, but it is also indebted to a visual grammar of Gothic monstrousness that developed in the second half of the eighteenth century. Artists from Goya to Fuseli found, in the emerging literature of the Gothic, images for fears that were unpaintable, and ways of representing ideas that were unsayable. Goya's 1799 aquatint etching *The Sleep of Reason Produces Monsters* (Plate 43 from 'Los Caprichos') shows the artist asleep, prey to the dark forces that arise when sleep descends and reason relaxes its vigilance (fig. 6). The unconscious artist slumbers in the foreground while shadowy bats and owls circle over him, both products of and threats to his vision. In Henry Fuseli's *The Nightmare* the threat of the monstrous other takes on a more sexualized form, as a crowing incubus perches on the exposed chest of a sleeping woman. Fuseli's painting was the subject of appalled and fascinated public comment following its first exhibition in 1782 and continues to attract interest today because of its unsettling reading of the relationship between self and other (fig. 7).

This painterly, highly visual language for the unknowable, for powerful external forces and for phenomena that threaten the sanctity and security of the human body, finds its way into *Frankenstein* in the way the Creature is described. He is a composite figure, made from the bodies of others but also from contemporary depictions of monstrousness, from which he derives his yellow skin and his exaggerated, elongated features. To describe him is almost beyond the power of language, as Frankenstein himself acknowledges.

5. Illustration of Coleridge's *Christabel* showing the temptress Geraldine standing over the reclining heroine. From *The Blue Poetry Book* by Andrew Lang; illustrations by H.J. Ford and L. Speed, 1891.

El sueño de la razon produce monstruos.

6. Francisco de Goya, *El Sueño de la Razon Produce Monstruos (The Sleep of Reason Produces Monsters)*, etching and aquatint, 1799.

7. Henry Fuseli, *The Nightmare*, 1781. Fuseli's depiction of monstrousness remains one of the most famous and unsettling visualisations of the Gothic tradition on which Mary drew.

How, he asks, to 'delineate the wretch whom with such infinite pains and care I had endeavoured to form? ... His yellow skin scarcely covered the work of muscles and arteries beneath; his hair was of a lustrous black, and flowing; his teeth of a pearly whiteness; but these luxuriances only formed a more horrid contrast with his watery eyes, that seemed almost of the same colour as the dun white sockets in which they were set, his shrivelled complexion, and straight black lips.'[9] Mary draws here too on Milton's description of Satan in *Paradise Lost*, in which Satan is famously described through synecdoche, as an indescribable composite of his parts.

Images of monstrous others had political as well as artistic resonances in 1816. In its depiction of both the possibility and danger of human agency, *Frankenstein* offers a response to the two revolutions that reshaped Mary's world. Her political sensibilities were inculcated in the shadow of the French Revolution of 1789: an event which her parents' generation had viewed as a glorious dawn but which, in the following decades, assumed a darker, more menacing aspect. Two caricatures published twenty years apart illustrate both this shift and the metaphorical power of monstrousness for Revolutionary commentators. *L'Hydre Aristocratique*, an anonymous French cartoon of 1789, depicts a battle between an aristocratic monster and the citizen liberators of the Bastille: the hydra is flailing and dying, assailed from all sides by the soldiers of freedom (fig. 8). In George Cruikshank's *Radical Reformer* of 1819, in contrast, it is the Revolutionaries who are monstrous: represented by a fire-breathing, animated guillotine, they

8. Anon, *L'Hydre Aristocratique* (1789), in which the aristocratic monster of the title is decapitated by the French citizenry under the shadow of the Bastille.

9. George Cruikshank, *A Radical Reformer, (ie) a Neck or Nothing Man! Dedicated to the Heads of the Nation*, 1819. In Cruikshank's image it is the Revolution itself that is monstrous: here an animated guillotine puts a group of gentlemen to flight.

threaten the peace and security of Britain (fig. 9). *Frankenstein* in its turn constructs an allegory for the French Revolution in which first the potential and then the vainglorious corruption of Revolutionary ambition is laid bare. The novel reacts too to the mechanization of the Industrial Revolution, and to its unlooked-for impact on labouring communities. The newspapers and periodicals of Mary's adolescence carried stories of Luddite frame-breakers alongside accounts of scientific innovation, and in *Frankenstein* she makes the corollary between experimentation and human cost brutally explicit even as she acknowledges the epoch-making promise of invention.

Frankenstein has sometimes been described as an early work of science fiction. In fact the novel gives very little away about the mechanics of the Creature's animation (something twentieth-century cinematic adaptations sought to redress). Mary's 1831 Introduction nevertheless offers a wealth of further evidence about the scientific ideas percolating as she began to write. The second half of the eighteenth century witnessed a series of ground-breaking investigations into the origins of life, from which Mary drew inspiration for her own exploration of the consequences of reanimation. In the Introduction she recalls Byron and Shelley talking about the pioneering work on spontaneous animation of Erasmus Darwin, although she adds a caveat: 'I speak not of what the Doctor really did, or said that he did, but, as more to my purpose, of what was then spoken of as having been done by him.' Darwin, she wrote, was said to have 'preserved a piece of vermicelli in a glass case, till by some extraordinary means it began to move with voluntary motion'.[10] Like so much else in the Introduction, Mary's reference to Darwin has been endlessly discussed and analysed by literary scholars. Her qualification ('I speak not of what the Doctor really did') offers fertile ground for investigation, as does her apparent compression of the activities of Darwin and the Italian physician Luigi Galvani. The compression illustrates the artistry of the Introduction, in which a swirl of competing ideas is honed and polished into a series of short anecdotes.

10. Illustration from Luigi Galvani, *De Viribus Electricitatis in Motu Musculari Commentarius* (1791) showing several pairs of frogs' legs in varying states of animation.

In disentangling this particular anecdote, it is possible to identify three interconnected strands of influence on the science of *Frankenstein*. The first and most obvious is the work of Galvani, who discovered that he could make the legs of a dead frog twitch with an electrical spark (fig. 10). Galvani's nephew, Giovanni Aldini, extended his uncle's work by attempting to resurrect not frogs but hanged criminals, although his efforts met with less success. Various demonstrations of the use and power of the galvanic battery were staged in Britain and Europe throughout Mary's childhood and adolescence, and were widely reported in the periodicals she read.

Although neither Galvani nor the generation of experimental electromagnetists who followed him were able to reanimate living creatures through the power of electricity, their efforts nevertheless called into question a centuries-old orthodoxy about the origins of life. So too did the work of the anatomists, whose apparent disregard for the sanctity of the human body was the cause of a fascinated horror reflected in both image and print (fig. 11). *Frankenstein* embraces the creative possibility offered by the end of this orthodoxy, both in its implicit and explicit allusions to Galvani and electricity, and in its engagement with other explorers of the limits of human knowledge. Erasmus Darwin was one such explorer, whose work on the origins of life and a proto-theory of evolution presaged the discoveries of his grandson Charles. In his *Temple of Nature*, published in 1803, Darwin went in search of what he called the 'spirit of animation' or vital principle: the animating spark that characterized living organisms (fig. 12). He developed a 'theory of spontaneous vitality' and argued that the source of this spirit or principle was material:[11] that it emerged in and was composed of matter. He also noted that dead matter might

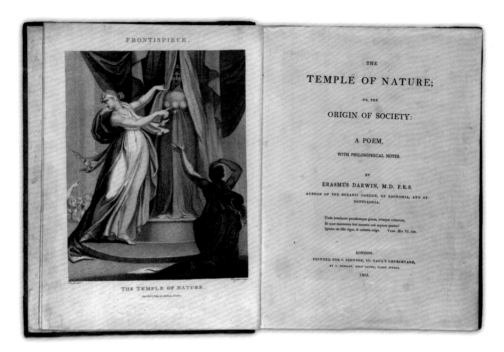

11. William Hogarth, *Fourth Stage of Cruelty: The Reward of Cruelty* (1751), in which the anatomists' lack of respect for the human form is everywhere apparent.

12. Frontispiece and title page of Erasmus Darwin's *The Temple of Nature*, 1803. This was the work in which Darwin explored the 'spirit of animation' and described the experiments with vermicelli discussed by Mary in her Introduction.

be reanimated by water, and it is this observation to which Mary refers in the Introduction:

> Thus the vorticella or wheel animal, which is found in rain water that has stood some days in leaden gutters, or in hollows of lead on the tops of houses, or in the slime or sediment left by such water, though it discovers no sign of life except when in the water, yet it is capable of continuing

alive for many months though kept in a dry state. In this state it is of a globulous shape, exceeds not the bigness of a grain of sand, and no signs of life appear; but being put into water, in the space of half an hour a languid motion begins, the globule turns itself about, lengthens itself by slow degrees, assumes the form of a lively maggot, and most commonly in a few minutes afterwards puts out its wheels, swimming vigorously through the water as if in search of food.[12]

Darwin paints an arresting image of suspended animation, and of a moment of apparently spontaneous reanimation. Again, though, his influence on *Frankenstein* lies not just in what he wrote, but in what his work appeared to promise. Mary emphasizes that at the Villa Diodati Shelley and Byron discussed not just the details of Darwin's writing but 'what was then spoken of as having been done by him', so in her account Darwin, like Galvani before him, comes to stand for a culture in which the most basic principles of life suddenly became fit and urgent subjects for wider discussion. In 1817 a very public version of an ongoing argument about the origins of life erupted between the Shelleys' doctor William Lawrence and John Abernethy, President of the Royal College of Surgeons. The debate rapidly became framed in political terms, as Abernethy argued that the vital spark of life came not from matter but from a divine, external power, and Lawrence countered with a materialist rebuttal in which life was posited as a force generated by a complex cycle of birth, generation and decay. Their confrontation was played out in the pages of periodicals and Lawrence was attacked as a blasphemous and seditious traitor who, in denying the supremacy of a God-given, vital spark, denied simultaneously hierarchies, the established order and all the forces that stood between Britain and the anarchy of revolution.

Frankenstein takes its spark, then, not from the specifics of these debates about the origins of life, but from their very presence in the public consciousness. The novel is also indebted to other accounts of scientific progress and discovery. Captain Cook's thwarted 1776 attempt to circumnavigate North America from the Pacific is rewritten in the story of Walton the explorer, whose narrative frames Frankenstein's and who offers a further cautionary tale about the dangers of overweening ambition. Walton's project, Marilyn Butler has noted, is 'eyecatching, real-life and up-to-the-minute, as Frankenstein's seemingly archaic, idiosyncratic enterprise is not'.[13] Cook's attempt faltered at the Bering Strait between Russia and North America, where his attempt to chart the Northwest Passage was thwarted by impassable ice floes. He died during the homeward voyage and his battle with the elements in the Bering Strait was later memorialized by artists and in the pages of the press. The Napoleonic Wars closed the seas to explorers for a generation but from 1817 onwards new attempts at Arctic exploration began once more to be reported. Writing in the *Quarterly Review*, John Wilson Croker presented the Arctic as thoroughly overcrowded in order to mock *Frankenstein*'s topicality. The Creature, Croker wrote, 'resolves to fly to the most inaccessible point of the earth; and, as our Review had not yet enlightened mankind upon the real state of the North Pole, he directs his course thither as a sure place of solitude and security'.[14]

Walton finds neither solitude nor security in his exploration of the Arctic, however, and the novel ends with him forced to confront the bitterness of his failure. As the ice thickens around his ship, threatening the lives of all aboard, he turns back at the insistence of his crew. 'The die is cast; I have consented to return,' he writes.

'Thus are my hopes blasted by cowardice and indecision; I come back ignorant and disappointed. It requires more philosophy than I possess, to bear this injustice with patience.'[15] When she revised the novel in 1831 Mary Shelley softened the anger of Walton's defeat, giving him new words in which he acknowledges his responsibility to his men. But in 1818 when the Arctic appeared still as a new frontier in the pursuit of knowledge she offered no amelioration, leaving Walton thwarted in the frozen wastes. Frankenstein dies aboard Walton's ship; the Creature disappears into a bleak wasteland to construct his own funeral pyre. Walton is forced to give up his dreams of glory and in the novel's closing pages his fate remains uncertain. Explorer, Creator and Creature reach the end of their stories trapped in a landscape no human ambition can overcome. The novel concludes with a sharp rebuke to egotism, in which the adventures of contemporary explorers come to stand as an epitaph for both the possibility and the folly of its author's historical moment: thus it offers a kaleidoscopic, multi-layered account of its time before leaving its characters and its readers marooned amidst the ice.

13. Tobias Conrad Lotter, *Carte de l'Océan Pacifique au nord de l'equateur, et des côtes qui le bornent des deux côtés: d'après les dernieres découvertes faites par les Espagnols, les Russes et les Anglois, jusqu'en 1780*, 1781. This was the first published map to show the route taken by Cook on his third voyage (1776–80).

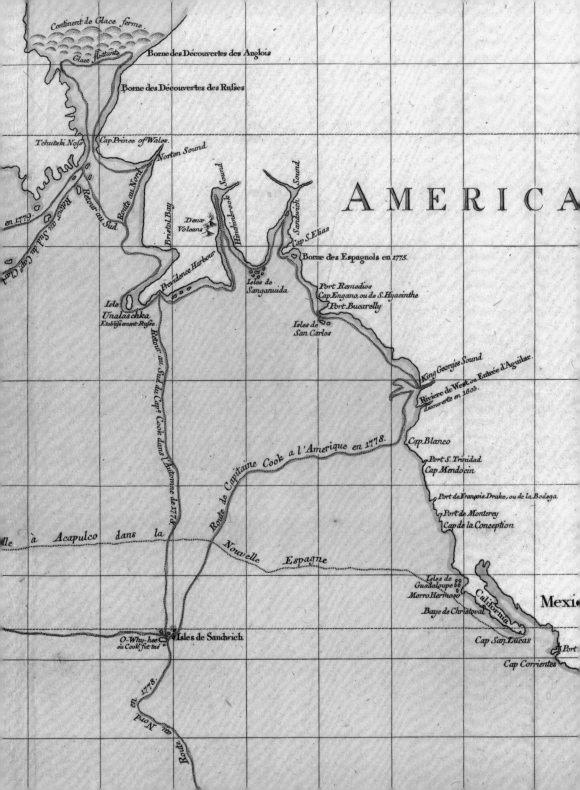

Continent de Glace ferme

Glace flottante

Borne des Découvertes des Anglois

Borne des Découvertes des Russes

Tchutzki Noss

Cap Prince of Wales.

Norton Sound

en 1779.

Retour au Sud.

Route au Nord

Bristol Bay

Providence Harbour

Deux Volcans

Hinchinbrook Sound

Sandwich Sound

Cap S. Elias

Borne des Espagnols en 1775.

AMERICA

Isle Unalaschka
Etablissement Russe

Retour au Sud du Cap. Cook dans l'Automne de 1778.

Isles de Sanganuida

Port Remedios
Cap. Engano, ou de S. Hyacinthe
Port Bucarelly

Isles de San Carlos

King Georges Sound

Riviere de West ou Entrée d'Aguilar.
découverte en 1603.

Route de Capitaine Cook a l'Amerique en 1778.

Cap Blanco

Port S. Trinidad
Cap Mendocin

Port de François Drake, ou de la Bodega

Port de Monterey
Cap de la Conception

lle à Acapulco dans la

Nouvelle Espagne

Isles de Guadaloupe
Morro Hermoso

Baye de Christoval

California

Mexic

O-Why-hee
ou Cook fut tué

Isles de Sandwich

Cap San Lucas

Port

1778

Route du Nord en

Cap Corrientes

2

PEOPLE

Who was the eighteen-year-old in whose imagination these ideas and images coalesced? And who were the people she lived amongst as she read and wrote? She was born in 1797, the only child to result from the union of William Godwin and Mary Wollstonecraft. Her birth made her the unwitting epitome of a radical idea: the personification of the unconventional union of two extraordinary thinkers. Godwin was a philosopher and the author of *Political Justice*: one of the most important works of radical political thought to emerge from the French Revolution. Wollstonecraft was a novelist, political campaigner, educationalist, historian and translator, although she is chiefly remembered now as the author of the founding text of the feminist movement, *A Vindication of the Rights of Woman*. Wollstonecraft died ten days after giving birth to Mary, as a result of septicaemia brought on by a retained placenta. Godwin recorded her death in his diary (fig. 15) in a note of elliptical bleakness: '20 minutes before 8'. Mary spent her childhood first in the company of her half-sister, Fanny Imlay (Wollstonecraft's daughter from a previous relationship) and then, after Godwin remarried, amongst a group of

14. Portrait of William Godwin by James Northcote, 1802.

20 minutes before 8. _____

Montagu, M, miss G & Fanny dine.
Carlisle calls: Montagu at tea.

Johnson & H n call: Montagu & miss G at tea.

H n, Opie n & Dyson n call: mrs removes: Fenwicks sup from Fordyce: write to Inchbald, Tuthil & Pares.

Write to mrs Cotton. Barbauld on Devotion, p. 22. Fenwicks & PV sup.

Funeral: M's lodgings. Write to Carlisle. Pursley, p. 50. Fawcet dines; adv. Fenwicks.

Pursley, p. 186: Mary, p. 187, fin. Call on Mkeveley, w. Fenwick: Fawcet dines: Fanny at home: H calls.

15. Page from William Godwin's diary for September 1797. The entry at the top of the page records the time of Wollstonecraft's death.

16. Portrait of Mary Wollstonecraft by John Opie, 1797. Wollstonecraft was pregnant with Mary when she was painted by Opie.

17. Posthumous portrait of Mary Shelley by Reginald Easton.

children who all had different parents. The second Mrs Godwin had two children of her own, Claire and Charles, by two fathers, and Godwin and his new wife had one child of their own, a boy called William. It was a strange household in which to be a small girl: Wollstonecraft's portrait hung in Godwin's study throughout his second marriage and he was a serious, sober man, more accustomed to thinking and writing than to looking after children. Samuel Taylor Coleridge, not a notably frivolous figure himself, wrote that he found 'the cadaverous Silence of Godwin's Children ... quite catacomb-ish'.[1]

As Mary entered adolescence her relationship with her stepmother became increasingly combustible and unhappy. In an attempt to restore some harmony to his home, Godwin sent Mary away to stay with friends in Scotland. She arrived home in the early summer of 1814 with a striking tartan skirt and an amalgam of new ideas in her head. In the Introduction to *Frankenstein* she described herself as 'the daughter of two persons of distinguished literary celebrity' born with the urge to write.[2] She evoked the memory of her Scottish residence, recalling 'the blank and dreary northern shores of the Tay'. 'Dreary on retrospection,' she continued. 'They were not so to me then. They were the eyry of freedom, and the pleasant region where unheeded I could commune with the creatures of my fancy.'[3] From Dundee she watched the great whaling ships venture out into the Atlantic and in the countryside around the Tay she found a landscape to which she would return when, in *Frankenstein*, she needed to create a landscape where both Frankenstein and the Creature could meet away from the bustle of society.

When Mary returned to London in the summer of 1814 it was to find that the poet Percy Bysshe Shelley had taken up residence as her father's chief disciple. Shelley was twenty-two in 1814 and was living apart from his pregnant wife Harriet and their baby. He had already been expelled from Oxford for writing (and refusing to admit to) the pamphlet 'The Necessity of Atheism', had published his visionary poem *Queen Mab*, which came complete with notes on religion, marriage and much else besides, and had made various attempts at inciting political action. He was estranged from his parents as well as from his wife, and was an isolated figure in search of people with whom he could exchange ideas and from whom he might receive sympathy and friendship. In sixteen-year-old Mary he found the embodiment of an ideal. The pair conducted a rapid courtship through stolen meetings at Wollstonecraft's grave in Old St Pancras Churchyard, and on 28 July 1814 they eloped to France, taking Mary's stepsister, Claire, with them. Mary became pregnant almost immediately after the elopement, but her daughter died a few days after her premature birth (fig. 19).

These events and their aftermath have been the subject of analysis, speculation and biographical commentary since the mid-nineteenth century. The elopement threw Shelley, Mary and Claire together as an unconventional family unit which was both imaginatively productive and intensely frustrating for all concerned. All three understood themselves to be living beyond the pale: they were barred from Godwin's home in Skinner Street and chased from lodging to lodging by bailiffs trying to recoup Shelley's debts. In their isolation they developed a shared language for their exile, which would reappear in striking ways in *Frankenstein*. In 1815 Shelley and Mary visited Oxford in the company of Claire's brother Charles: writing to his sister afterwards, Charles reported on their visit in the following terms:

18. Portrait of Claire Clairmont by Amelia Curran, 1819. Claire disliked this image (the only likeness taken in her lifetime) intensely.

I and my baby go about 3 – I do
do not come till six – Hogg comes
in the evening
     Friday 3d
nurse my baby – talk & read
Lormne Hogg comes in the evening
     Saturday 4th
read talk and nurse – I read
the life of Chaucer Hogg comes
in the evening & sleeps –
     Sunday 5 –
I & S go to town – Hogg here
all day read Lormne & nurse
my baby – in the evening talk
S finishes the life of Chau
cer – H. goes at 11
     Monday 6th
find my baby dead –
Send for Hogg – talk – a
miserable day – in the eve

19. Page from Mary Shelley's diary for 6 March 1815. A series of entries recording the early days of her infant daughter's life ('I and my baby go about 3', 'nurse my baby', 'talk and nurse', 'nurse my baby') give way at the bottom of a page to a bleak sentence: 'find my baby dead'.

We visited the very rooms where [Shelley] ... poured with the incessant & unwearied application of an Alchemyst over the artificial & natural boundaries of human knowledge; brooded over the perceptions which were the offspring of their villainous & impudent penetration & even dared to threaten the World with the horrid & diabolical project of telling mankind to <u>open its eye</u>.[4]

This highly wrought account of the undergraduate Shelley pursuing chemical experiments under the noses of the disapproving Fellows of his College delights in its construction of Shelley as a figure operating outside society, motivated by the pursuit of knowledge rather than the petty dictates of convention. A year later, writing to Lord Byron, Claire made the following plea: 'The Creator ought not to destroy his Creature.'[5] Again this is suggestive of a shared linguistic register, used here by Claire in an attempt to hold Byron to her and then later by Mary in *Frankenstein* as she developed the conceptual framework in which the novel's narrative of egotism, responsibility and exile unfolds.

In the Genevan summer of 1816 Mary began work on *Frankenstein* amidst a hubbub of voices. The rhythm of her days was punctuated by conversations: with Shelley (and sometimes Byron) over breakfast; with an assortment of companions during afternoon boating expeditions on the lake; and then, when the weather turned, during stormy evenings at the Villa Diodati. Writing in her journal a few months after Shelley's death, Mary presented an account of these evenings in which she figured as the silent auditor of the conversational fireworks of Shelley and Byron. It seems likely that there is a degree of revisionism in her presentation of memory, since her journal entries for this period are overwhelmingly concerned with celebrating Shelley at her own

20. Engraving of the Villa Diodati from E. Finden, *Diodati, the Residence of Lord Byron*, 1833, pp. 90–1.

expense. Nevertheless, she subsequently chose to encode this version of the conversational dynamics of the Diodati coterie in print as well, when she presented herself as a witness to the conversations of others. 'I do not think that any person's voice has the same power of awakening melancholy in me as Albe's,' she wrote in her journal, using an old nickname for Byron. 'I have been accustomed when hearing it to listen & to speak little; – another voice, not mine, ever replied, a voice whose strings are broken; and when Albè ceases to speak I expect to hear <u>that other</u> voice, & when I hear another instead, it jars strangely with every association.' 'When Albe speaks', she continued, '& Shelley does not answer, it is as thunder without rain, The form of the sun without heat or light.' In the journal she attributed her own silence to 'incapacity & timidity', a self-presentation that sits uneasily against other characterizations of her.[6] Much has been written about the mutually productive exchange of ideas between Shelley and Byron during this period; less frequently commented upon is the extent to which Byron was struck by Mary's conversation. Many years later he recalled how much she impressed him, telling one of his biographers 'Mrs Shelley is very clever.' Like Shelley he was impressed not just by what Mary said but by the radical glamour of her birth: 'indeed it would be difficult for her not to be so; the daughter of Mary Wollstonecraft and Godwin ... could be no common person.'[7]

Frankenstein offers an additional way to read Mary's self-described silence. The novel is characterized by what narrative theorists have termed 'heteroglossia': literally, different tongues, or language. Many scholars have argued that it embeds critical portraits of Byron and Shelley in its depiction of the egotistical, overweening artist. Of greater significance though is the way in which the novel reworks the voices of Shelley and Byron, as well as those of Claire and Charles Clairmont, in its multivalent account of creativity. The story itself is told by a tangle of voices: Walton, Frankenstein, the Creature and Elizabeth all narrate at different points. The language it deploys to critique prejudice and reactions to difference is drawn too from the tangle of voices around Mary, and much of the novel's power comes from the way in which she adapts the language of others for her own purposes.

Shelley and Byron were not the only members of the Diodati party engaged in conversations about the origins of life that summer. In the diary he kept at the time, Byron's doctor John Polidori recorded that it was he who engaged in debates with Shelley about 'principles ... whether man was to be thought merely an instrument'. In another diary entry he noted an evening spent talking 'till the ladies' brains whizzed with giddiness about idealism'.[8] In her Introduction Mary excised Polidori from the account of *Frankenstein*'s originary conversation, and it seems likely that Polidori indulged in some self-aggrandizement in a diary he kept with a view to publication. Nevertheless, he was the only member of the party with a medical training and his own work placed him at the forefront of scientific investigations into altered states of consciousness. He had written a doctoral thesis at the University of Edinburgh on somnambulism and was well-versed in contemporary debates about materialism, vitality and the autonomy of man. By the time Mary wrote her Introduction Polidori was dead by his own hand, and she may have wanted to distinguish his work and reputation from her own. Polidori produced his own response to the ghost story competition in a story he published in 1819, *The Vampyre* (fig. 21). *The Vampyre* is sometimes grouped with *Frankenstein*, but in reality the two works have few similarities. However, Polidori's story plays a small but important role in the history of the Gothic, introducing the vampire as one of its stock characters, and both works share a preoccupation with otherness: with figures who sit outside the confines of society and who threaten disruption through their very being.

It is possible to detect the voice of one more visitor to the Villa Diodati in *Frankenstein*. Byron's friend Matthew Lewis was the author of *The Monk*, a notoriously violent tale of demons and horror published in 1796, and he was also, through inheritance, the owner of a Jamaican plantation and 400 slaves. As a slave owner he was in favour not

THE

VAMPYRE;

A Tale.

LONDON:

PRINTED FOR SHERWOOD, NEELY, AND JONES,
PATERNOSTER-ROW.

———

1819.

[Entered at Stationers' Hall, March 27, 1819.]

250. a. 317.

21. Title page for Polidori's *The Vampyre*, 1819.

22. Wedgwood Committee for Abolition medallion, 'Am I not a man and a brother', *c.1787.*

of abolition but of amelioration and when he arrived in Geneva he engaged in heated argument about the slave trade with Byron's neighbour Madame de Staël. *Frankenstein* offers an explicit challenge to the slave trade through its unsparing investigation of the consequences of treating an individual as less human because of his physical characteristics. It thus stands as a rebuttal to Lewis's arguments for amelioration over abolition by refuting otherness as legitimate grounds for the practice of social difference and it highlights the immorality of Lewis's position through its presentation of Frankenstein's warped perception of his Creature. Mary and Shelley's joint diary for the period records too that Lewis's arrival in Geneva triggered a further round of ghost stories at Diodati. 'He told us four other stories,' Shelley wrote. 'All grim.'[9]

Frankenstein, though, is not shaped only by those in Mary's circle who spoke loudest. It also demonstrates a deep preoccupation with the stories of those who cannot speak, or who speak but are not heard. At the end of August 1816, Shelley, Mary and Claire left Switzerland to return to England. There they faced an uncertain future. Claire's pregnancy made any reconciliation with Godwin impossible so rather than return to London they took lodgings in Bath, far away from the suspicious eye of parents and step-parents. Byron had undertaken to provide for Claire's unborn child, but only by offering to take the child into his own establishment at a time of his choosing. As they settled into their Bath lodgings, therefore, Shelley, Mary and Claire all knew that the baby Claire was carrying would remain hers only for as long as Byron chose to permit. This claustrophobic family grouping had already lost one baby with the death of Mary's premature daughter in 1815; now they had to confront a future in which they would be compelled to relinquish another child. Mary gave the name of her second baby (a son called William, born in January 1816) to Frankenstein's younger brother, a beloved child who is snatched from his family and murdered in the Creature's first act of revenge. The loss of a child and the rights and responsibilities of the parent: these are the central themes of *Frankenstein*, and they owe their genesis to the domestic circumstances of the novel's composition.

Frankenstein's engagement with the consequences of parenthood is formal as well as thematic. It took Mary nine months to write the novel, and for several of those months she was pregnant with her third child, a girl born in September 1817. The framing narrative of Walton's journey also takes place over a nine-month period, between 11 December and 12 September. It thus almost exactly mirrors the period in which

Mary's mother, Mary Wollstonecraft, became pregnant and gave birth to Mary, and Walton's final letter is dated two days after the date on which Wollstonecraft died. Mary grew up with the knowledge that her birth caused her mother's death and she writes this story into *Frankenstein* through the medium of dates on letters, further intertwining the stories of creativity and responsibility enmeshed in both the novel and the story of its birth.

In the autumn of 1816, Shelley, Mary and Claire were assailed by a double tragedy. In October Mary's half-sister Fanny Imlay left Godwin's house in London and travelled by coach to Swansea. There she took an overdose of laudanum. 'I have long determined', she wrote to Godwin, 'that the best thing I could do was to put an end to the existence of a being whose birth was unfortunate, and whose life has only been a series of pain to those persons who have hurt their health in endeavouring to promote her welfare. Perhaps to hear of my death will give you pain, but you will soon have the blessing of forgetting that such a creature ever existed.'[10] The thematic cadences of Fanny's note reappear in the Creature's narrative in *Frankenstein*. He shares with her the pain of being unwanted, and of being born in misery; he also takes the dehumanized name she gave herself at the point of her death. 'Will no entreaties cause thee to turn a favourable eye upon thy creature?' he demands of his maker.[11] Mary's diary entries for the period of Fanny's suicide are clipped and brief, and in its aftermath she threw herself into work, writing the early chapters of *Frankenstein* at speed. Fanny had been the companion of Mary's infancy, and the joint

23. Portrait of William Shelley by Amelia Curran, 1819. Curran painted William shortly before his death, aged three.

Oct. 13, 1816

I did indeed expect it.

I cannot but thank you for your strong ex
pressions of sympathy. I do not see however that that
sympathy can be of any service to me: but it is best.

My advice, & earnest prayer is, that you
would avoid any thing that leads to Publicity. Go not
to Swansea. Disturb not the silent dead. Do nothing
to destroy the obscurity she so much desired, that now
rests upon the event. It was, as I said, her last wish.
It was the motive that led her from London to Bristol, & from Bristol to Swansea.

I said that your sympathy could be of
no service to me. But I retract the assertion. By ob
serving what I have just recommended to you, it
may be of infinite service. Think what is the situa-
tion of my wife & myself, now deprived of all our
children but the youngest; & do not expose us
to those idle questions, which to a mind in anguish
is one of the severest of all trials

We are at this moment in doubt whe-
ther during the first shock we shall not say that
she is gone to Holland to her aunts, a thing that

inheritor of Wollstonecraft's scandalous name. In early adulthood Mary found Fanny trying and dull, and she knew that Fanny had felt shut out from the apparently charmed circle around Shelley. But it was Fanny who walked through the rain to bring baby things following the birth of Mary's daughter, and Fanny who kept a fragile chain of communication open between Mary and Godwin. *Frankenstein* suggests that Mary understood Fanny's tragedy to be both a product of her birth and of her treatment by others, and that her suicide was a rebuke to those, including Mary and Shelley, who had sought to discount Fanny's voice and the validity of her emotional experience.

Less than three months later Mary and Shelley were confronted with another suicide note, this time by Shelley's estranged wife, Harriet. Harriet drowned herself in the Serpentine in December 1816, unable to bear her neglected life in the shadows any longer. In her final letter (fig. 25) she demanded that Shelley live up to the responsibility of caring for their young son Charles (their daughter, Ianthe, she wanted Shelley to leave in the care of her sister Eliza). 'As you form his infant mind', she warned, 'so you will reap the fruits hereafter.'[12] In the event the Lord Chancellor decided that Shelley was not fit to form the mind of any infant and deprived him of the custody of his children by Harriet: a rare case of the primacy of a father's rights to his children being overturned on the grounds of paternal unfitness. Charles and Ianthe Shelley thus join the group of children who were

24. William Godwin's letter to Shelley of 13 October 1816, written following the news of Fanny Imlay's suicide and illustrating that Godwin feared the worst when Fanny disappeared. 'I did indeed expect it,' he writes. 'I cannot but thank you for your strong expressions of sympathy. I do not see however that that sympathy can be of any service to me: but it is best.'

lost to Mary, Shelley and Claire during the period of *Frankenstein's* composition.

Harriet's declaration of parental responsibility has its inverse counterpart in the novel, which deals with the disasters that unfold as a neglectful parent reaps the fruits of his actions. 'No father had watched my infant days,' the Creature laments. 'No mother had blessed me with smiles and caresses.'[13] Elsewhere he reprimands Frankenstein in language derived from Milton: 'I am thy creature: I ought to be thy Adam; but I am rather the fallen angel, whom thou drivest from joy for no misdeed.'[14] To be driven from joy and from human companionship, to be marginalized and scorned: this is the fate that befalls the Creature, and which prompts him to enact a terrible revenge. His story makes clear the rights of the marginalized to be heard, be they slaves, women or children. Finally, it is their voices that are heard through him as he conjures a vision of his funeral pyre. 'I shall die,' he proclaims:

> I shall no longer feel the agonies which now consume me, or be the prey of feelings unsatisfied, yet unquenched. He is dead who called me into being; and when I shall be no more, the very remembrance of us both will speedily vanish. I shall no longer see the sun or stars, or feel the winds play on my cheeks. Light, feeling, and sense, will pass away; and in this condition must I find my happiness.[15]

25. Harriet Shelley's suicide note, December 1816. 'do not regret the loss of one who could never be anything but a source of vexation & misery to you all,' she writes. 'Too wretched to exert myself lowered in the opinion of everyone why should I drag on a miserable existence embittered by past recollections & not one ray of hope to rest on for the future.'

To you my dear Sister I leave all my things as they more
properly belong to you than any one I you will preserve them
for Ianthe Goubazgi botto. My dearest L Mucthbel Sister

When you read this lett. I shall be more an inhabi
-tant of this miserable world. do not regret the loss of one who could
never be anything but a source of vexation & misery to you all belong
-ing to me. I've wretched to exert myself towered in the opinion of
everyone why that I drag on a miserable existence embittered
by past recollections And one ray of hope to rest on for the
future. The remembrance of all your kindness which I have
so unworthily repaid has often made my heart ache. I know
that you will forgive me because it is not in your
nature to be unkind to any. Dear amiable
woman that I had never left you Oh! that I had always
taken your advice. I might have lived long & happy
but alas I wilfully have rushed on my own destruction
I have not written to Byffke. And what would it avail
my wishes or my prayers would not be attended to by him
& yet I should like see this perhaps he might grant my
last request to let Ianthe remain with you always
dear lovely child, with you she will enjoy much happiness
with him none. My dear Byffke let me conjure
you by the remembrance of our days of happiness to
grant my last wish do not take your innocent child
from Ely & & ho her been more than I know, who her
watched over her with such unceasing care. Do not refuse
my last request I never could refuse you. if you had
never left me I might have lived but now in I freely forgive
you & may you enjoy that happiness which you have denied
me &c.

3
PLACE

On 10 April 1815 the Indonesian volcano Mount Tambora erupted. It blasted gas, dust and rock into the atmosphere, killed tens of thousands of people and altered the climate of the northern hemisphere for years. In England, Turner was inspired by sunsets of violent red; on the shores of Lake Geneva the sun failed to come out at all. It is for this reason that 1816 is sometimes referred to as 'the year without a summer'. In the mythology of *Frankenstein* a neat line has been drawn between Tambora's eruption and the storms that drove Mary, Shelley and Byron inside to tell ghost stories, and the metaphor of *Frankenstein* as volcanic matter does indeed have an irresistible quality.

Volcanologists now know that the 1815 eruption of Mount Tambora was the most violent explosion to have occurred on our planet in the last 10,000 years. But in 1816 the inhabitants of the Villa Diodati had no idea why the sun had been so summarily extinguished. News of Tambora travelled slowly and it was many years before nineteenth-century scientists began to connect the explosion to the changes in

26. J.M.W. Turner, *Red Sky and Crescent Moon*, c.1818 (detail). This is one of a number of works in which Turner captured the extraordinary red skies and sunsets produced by the aftermath of Tambora's eruption.

weather patterns, failed harvests and spread of disease which followed in its wake. Writing to Fanny in June 1816, Mary could only report that summer and winter appeared to be warring for supremacy in the Swiss sky:

> An almost perpetual rain confines us principally to the house; but when the sun bursts forth it is with a splendour and heat unknown in England. The thunder storms that visit us are grander and more terrific than I have ever seen before. We watch them as they approach from the opposite side of the lake, observing the lightning play among the clouds in various parts of the heavens, and dart in jagged figures upon the piny heights of Jura, dark with the shadow of the overhanging cloud, while perhaps the sun is shining cheerily upon us.[1]

Mary's letter illustrates that Tambora's impact on *Frankenstein* was not restricted to its imposition of rainy-day activities on the Diodati circle. The lightning she watched dance around Lake Geneva appears in the novel in split form. Early in the novel it figures as inspiration for the galvanic spark that animates the Creature as Frankenstein observes a storm advance from behind the mountains of Jura and witnesses a lightning bolt destroy an old and beautiful oak tree. 'The catastrophe of this tree excited my extreme astonishment,' he recalls. 'I eagerly inquired of my father the nature and origin of thunder and lightning. He replied "Electricity", describing at the same time the various effects of that power.'

Later in the novel Frankenstein arrives at night outside the gates of Geneva and is caught in a storm. As he watches lightning reverberate around the lake it suddenly – and horrifyingly – endows him with vision:

A flash of lightning illuminated the object, and discovered its shape plainly to me; its gigantic stature, and the deformity of its aspect, more hideous than belongs to humanity, instantly informed me that it was the wretch, the filthy daemon to whom I had given life. What did he there? Could he be ... the murderer of my brother?[2]

Lightning is figured here as a revelatory force that shows both the misshapen outline of the Creature and the web of self-deceit into which Frankenstein has fallen. This is no heroic battle with the elements: rather the elements confront Frankenstein, the 'Modern Prometheus' of the subtitle, with the consequences of his attempt to harness the power of nature for his own ends. By the shores of Lake Geneva Frankenstein is shown the fatal folly of his visions, amidst the landscape in which his creator's imagination took flight. This complicated interplay between fiction and reality is typical of Mary's narrative dexterity. In this moment she treats the landscape around her as more than source or setting, making it instead an idea which unites the novel's intertwined strands of commentary on creativity, egotism and community. Frankenstein ends his days cast out into the landscape, barred as surely as his Creature by his own actions from the sociable community of which the Villa Diodati is emblematic. In Geneva Mary found conversation and friendship, and she subsequently recalled windy evenings on the lake during which Byron sang wild Albanian songs as she gloried in the sensation of being entangled in a contest with the elements. She shared her enthusiasm with Shelley, who scattered sketches of sailing boats throughout his notebooks (fig. 28). Many years later, writing after Shelley's death and of a period when she herself was ill and fearful, she recalled the peace that came to her aboard Shelley's boat, 'when lying down with my head on his knees

27. Percy Bysshe Shelley, view across Lake Geneva.

28. Percy Bysshe Shelley, sketches of sailing boats.

I shut my eyes & felt the wind & our swift motion alone'.[3] *Frankenstein*, however, she set adrift without the consolation of company and the novel's final image is of the Creature leaping away from a community of men onto an ice-raft. Thus, as the story ends, he is 'borne away by the waves, and lost in darkness and distance'.[4]

A lightning-framed lake is not the only element of the Swiss landscape to appear in *Frankenstein*. The novel also testifies to the deep and profound influence of Mont Blanc on the imaginations of both

901

Mary and Percy Shelley. The Shelleys visited Mont Blanc in July 1816 and spent several days exploring the countryside around Chamonix. On 25 July Mary recorded in her diary her impressions of the Mer de Glace, which in *Frankenstein* serves as the setting for the meeting between the Creator and his Creature. 'This is the most desolate place in the world,' she wrote. 'Iced mountains surround it – no sign of vegetation appears except on the place from which [we] view the ice – It is traversed by irregular crevices whose sides of ice appear blue while the surface is of a dirty white.'[5] This scene of majestic desolation serves in the novel to highlight Frankenstein's isolation by staging his encounter with the Creature away from the human realm of homes and cultivation in an unearthly landscape in which the grandeur of rock and ice appears to the fallible human eye as sea. The eerie beauty of the landscape offers Frankenstein a fleeting moment of joy before forcing him to confront the horror of his own making:

> A mist came over my eyes, and I felt a faintness seize me; but I was quickly restored by the cold gale of the mountains. I perceived, as the shape came nearer, (sight tremendous and abhorred!) that it was the wretch whom I had created.[6]

The elements force revelation, silhouetting the Creature against the whiteness, blowing new awareness into his deluded Creator. In a novel deeply interested in the pursuit of knowledge it is significant that self-knowledge is enabled by the natural world, which offers only a chimera of refuge for Frankenstein. In presenting this version of Mont Blanc in her novel, Mary was responding not only to the places she visited, but to Shelley's poetic instantiation of those places. He too wrote on Mont Blanc in the weeks following their travels, producing a poem fundamentally concerned with the relationship between place and knowledge. 'Mont Blanc' explores the space opened up by enquiries into the unseen power of nature and the limits of the human mind in relation to its inability to comprehend that power (fig. 30). 'And what were thou ...' Shelley asks the mountain in conclusion, 'If to the human mind's imaginings/ Silence and solitude were vacancy?'[7] *Frankenstein* takes up that question, investigating both the power of the human mind and the consequences of stripping away all affective connections, until ultimately Creator and Creature are bound together in a silent *pas de deux* of pursuit and isolation.

When Mary returned to England in September 1816 she took with her a collection of Swiss memories, along with early drafts of her story and a diary of her travels. The hard graft of turning that story into a full-length novel, however, took place in England: first in Bath, where Mary continued her working draft, and then at Albion House in Marlow, where she completed the draft and transcribed it into fair-copy before later correcting the proofs. In Bath Mary and Shelley took lodgings at 5 Abbey Churchyard and installed Claire in separate lodgings nearby in New Bond Street. Even with Claire living under a separate roof Mary found the claustrophobia of a Bath autumn difficult to tolerate. In the interstices of time between writing she took drawing lessons, read Davy's *Elements of Chemical Philosophy* and walked the streets. Sometimes she and Claire walked out into countryside where they were confronted with poverty and distress, the 'year without a summer' having resulted in a failed harvest in Britain and widespread rural hunger. The private disasters of Fanny and Harriet's suicides had their public corollary at the end of 1816 in unrest and rioting. In response to the Spa Fields riots of December 1816 the Tory government of Lord Liverpool introduced a raft

29. Charles Gore, *Chamonix, Mer de Glace*, 1778–9, showing the setting for Frankenstein's confrontation with the Creature.

Chamouny Glaciers

30. Page from Shelley's 'Mont Blanc' notebook, showing at the top an early experiment with the poem's concluding lines: 'When all the shapes/ If to the human minds imaginings/ Silence & solitude were vacancy.'

Sunday 21st July.
Heavy Showers.
JW served Maidford A. & Jan McKinley
FHW afternoon prayers and dined
J Wilson pd 20 on acct

	Bar	Ther	Wind
	29 2/10	64	S

Monday 22nd Showery.
Tom and Maria dined at Blakeley
Wine from Mr Hillyard, Northton
port eleven Bottles at
Cape Madeira thirteen Bottles at
John weeding.

| 29 1/10 | 64 | SW |

Tuesday 23rd Showery
Glyd came and dined. Do FHW.
Peas from Blakeley the first and
Do Cucumber !!
John odd jobs.

| 29 2/10 | 63 | SW |

Wednesday 24th Heavy Showers.
Glyd called and went home.
Glyd budded two Bullace Stocks planted
on SW side of House with apricots
Note fr: Mrs Hodgson.
John weeding. Thunder heard remote

| 29 2/10 | 65 | S |

Thursday 25th Heavy Showers.
Raked over some of the Hay in
Home close — spoiled by the Wet.
John absent.

| 29 3/10 | 66 | SW var |

Friday 26th Showery. Rain Bow vesp.
set out more annuals.
John weeding.

| 29 4/10 | 65 | W var |

Saturday 27th No rain !! the first
dry day for 24 Days.
Turned the remainder of the Hay in
close
John odd jobs pd John in full

| 29 3/10 | 64 | W |

31. Page from the Reverend Samson White's weather diary for July 1816, recording the heavy rain and wind that blighted the harvest in the year after the eruption of Mount Tambora.

of repressive legal measures designed to clamp down on opposition and debate. The disparity between the powerful and the marginalized was clear for all to see, but in Bath Mary and Shelley were uncharacteristically muted in their opposition, silenced by their distance from public events and by letters bringing news of personal tragedies. In December Mary wrote to Shelley in some desperation about his search for a house and her need to leave the misery of Bath behind her:

> Were you indeed a winged Elf and could soar over mountains & seas and could pounce on the little spot – A house with a lawn a river or lake – noble trees & divine mountains that should be our little mousehole to retire to. – But never mind this – give me a garden & <u>absentia Clariae</u> and I will thank my love for many favours.[8]

Mary did not achieve her wish for a house in 'absentia Clariae', but at the end of February 1817, after the birth of Claire's daughter by Byron, the Shelleys (now married to each other, following the death of Harriet) established their household at Albion House in Marlow. Claire and her baby remained with them, the future of the baby uncertain while they waited for instructions from Byron. In April the house was filled with more children, when Shelley's friend Leigh Hunt arrived with his family for an extended visit. Albion House offered Mary the possibility of peace and permanency, and a space in which she could think and write. The Shelleys' finances had stabilized courtesy of a negotiated settlement of Shelley's future inheritance, and the Hunts

32. Mary Shelley's travelling dressing case with mirror, which accompanied her on many of her later journeys.

were congenial company. Mary's diary records that she revised and transcribed *Frankenstein* amongst friends, interspersing sessions at her desk with walks with Shelley and Thomas Love Peacock, an old acquaintance and Buckinghamshire neighbour. There were boating expeditions and animated discussions of politics, the latter triggered by the stream of London newspapers sent down to Hunt each week.

It was a stimulating, congenial period, and when Mary gave birth to her daughter on 2 September (named Clara, to please Claire) the combination of the baby's birth and the recent completion of *Frankenstein* appeared to herald a more positive future.

Bath and Marlow play their part in the story of the composition of *Frankenstein* but neither place makes much impression on the narrative itself. Mary was no literalist in her evocation of place: indeed, the absence of the English towns in which she was living as she wrote the novel suggests that its rendering of the Swiss landscapes of the novel's genesis was deliberate rather than reflexive. Instead of writing about the places around her, she drew on the memories of places visited – or heard about – in her past. Frankenstein pauses on his travels through Britain in the Oxford of Shelley's youth and the London of Mary's childhood. In order to create a companion for his Creature he retreats to the Orkney Islands, onto which Mary transposed memories of North Sea vistas stemming from her adolescent residence outside Dundee. The Scottish landscape serves as a stage in the novel for the second confrontation between Frankenstein and the Creature which, like their first meeting on the slopes of Mont Blanc, takes place far away from centres of human habitation. In Scotland Frankenstein stands truly apart, shorn of companionship and context by the interplay between geography, action and imagination. 'In the evening', he writes, 'I walked on the stony beach of the sea, to listen to the waves as they roared, and dashed at my feet. It was a monotonous, yet ever-changing scene. I thought of Switzerland; it was far different from this desolate and appalling landscape. Its hills are covered with vines, and its cottages are scattered thickly in the plains. Its fair lakes reflect a blue and gentle sky; and when troubled by the winds, their tumult is

33. William Daniell, *The Snook at Hoy on Orkney*, from Richard Ayton, *A Voyage round Great Britain Undertaken in the Summer of the Year 1813*, 1813.

but as the play of a lively infant when compared to the roarings of the giant ocean.'⁹

As he gazes out into the North Sea Frankenstein becomes briefly the figure in Caspar David Friedrich's *Wanderer Above the Sea of Fog*, completed in the year of *Frankenstein*'s publication (fig. 34). He is the dreamer alone in the landscape, a representation of the myth of solitary creativity to which he also contributes. His, however, are the dreams of despair and his Creature lurks just out of sight, preventing him from taking solace in the scant consolations of isolation. Ultimately the novel's geography demolishes the romance of solitary creativity just as surely as the story, as it insists through its staging of confrontation that nature is not to be used as a retreat from the responsibilities of man. Frankenstein's Orkney solitude is disrupted by the appearance of the Creature, and by his realization that at every stage in his progress through Britain he has been followed by the embodiment of a disaster of his own making. 'He had followed me on my travels; he had loitered in forests, hid himself in caves, or taken refuge in wide and desert heaths.' The Creature wants the companion Frankenstein has promised: he realizes, unlike his Creator, that the promise of happiness lies not in landscapes but in people. 'You must create a female for me', he tells Frankenstein, 'with whom I can live in the interchange of those sympathies necessary for my being.'¹⁰ This is the drama that the novel stages: a conflict between community and isolation, between village and mountain. And as the story reaches its final sequence of tragedies it becomes clear that Romantic landscapes offer no consolation at all.

34. Caspar David Friedrich's *The Wanderer Above the Sea of Fog* (1818), the archetypal image of the isolated Romantic dreamer alone in the landscape.

Elizabeth For me ~~should be~~ ~~perfectly although the~~ ~~piece~~ was a great dissimilitude in our characters. I was more calm and philosophical than my companion yet I was not ~~so~~ so mild or yielding my application was of longer endurance but it was not so severe whilst it ~~lasted~~ my amusement ~~were studying old books of chemistry and natural magic those of Elizabeth drawing & music~~

~~When~~ I had My brothers were considerably younger than myself but I had a friend ~~who~~ ~~was~~ in one of my ~~own~~ fellows who compensated for this. ~~Clerval~~ was the son of a merchant of Geneva ~~and~~ an intimate friend of my father He was a boy of singular talent & fancy Immense when he was only nine years old he wrote a fairy tale which was the delight and amazement of all his companions. ~~His~~ favourite study consisted in books of romance when very young, I can and we used

Left margin:
~~there~~ & yet there was an harmony in that very dis- which We were strangers to any species of disunion or dispute

I delighted in investigating the facts relative to the actual world, she busied herself in the aerial creations of the poets. The world was to me a secret which I desired to disco- ver, — to her it was a ~~barren~~

4
PAPER

The notebooks in which Mary drafted and copied *Frankenstein* are owned by the Bodleian Library in Oxford. The remnants of four notebooks survive: two draft books, known as 'Draft Notebooks A and B', and two fair-copy volumes, known as 'Fair-Copy Notebooks C1 and C2'. In the decades since the notebooks were deposited at the Bodleian by Lord Abinger (the inheritor of many of the Shelleys' papers) successive generations of scholars have made the pilgrimage to Oxford to pore over the manuscripts, inspecting and noting every ink blot, doodle and deletion. Developments in technology mean that in the twenty-first-century scholars can perform much of this work from the comfort of their own computers, thanks first to Charles Robinson's magnificent facsimile edition of the manuscripts (published by Garland Press in 1996) and second to the online Shelley-Godwin Archive (http://shelleygodwinarchive.org/), which contains annotated photographs of each manuscript page. Neither facsimile nor online image, however, can quite prepare the reader for the raw physicality of the manuscript

35. Page from the *Frankenstein* manuscripts, Notebook A, illustrating the margins Mary ruled as she began work.

36. Beta radiograph of Britannia watermark in Notebook B, confirming the provenance of the second of the *Frankenstein* notebooks.

37. Photograph of the *Frankenstein* Notebook B showing the pages piled together in their original order.

itself. Seen in its papery flesh it appears as an artefact: an object which, like the Creature it describes, has taken on a life of its own.

We know from reading Mary's journal for 1816 that she began work on 'my story' during her Genevan summer. That story – sometimes referred to as the 'ur-text' for *Frankenstein* – is now lost, but before she left Geneva Mary purchased Notebook A: a bound book now comprising seventy-seven light-blue leaves of Continental make. Between late August and around December 1816 Mary rewrote her story into this notebook, expanding and revising as she went in order to transform her tale from a short work into a full-length novel. By late 1816 she had filled Notebook A and moved onto Notebook B: a book now containing seventy-five leaves of British-made paper, thicker and creamier than that of Notebook A. By April 1817, following the move to Albion House, she had finished the draft in Notebook B and returned to Notebook A, adding insertions on loose-leaf paper, and making corrections to the text. In both notebooks she ruled margins on the pages, thus leaving

herself plenty of space for revisions and alterations (fig. 35). She numbered the pages as she wrote and throughout the manuscript there are tallies of figures which suggest that as she wrote she was working out how many words she needed in order to produce a two- or three-volume novel. Once the draft was complete she began the laborious process of transcribing it into fair-copy for the printer. Fragments of the last two notebooks of fair-copy survive, called Notebooks C1 and C2, while the rest have disappeared.

In the summer of 1817 Shelley began negotiations with London publishers over *Frankenstein*, maintaining that he was acting on behalf of an anonymous young writer living abroad. In late August or early September 1817 he agreed a deal with the publisher Lackington and Co. in which Mary would receive a share of the profits, and in the early autumn of 1817, following the birth of Clara, Mary and Shelley appeared to have worked on the proofs together. The first edition of *Frankenstein* was published in January 1818 and through Shelley Mary ordered ten copies for herself, to be bound in boards. All the notebooks held by the Bodleian are disbound. The fair-copy was probably disassembled by the printers; the draft notebooks at an unknown date. The best approximation of the physicality of the notebooks in which Mary wrote is thus a set of photographs stored with the manuscripts, which show the pages piled as if for binding. The photographs were taken by Bodleian conservators before the manuscript leaves were individually mounted in the protective booklets (known as fascicules) in which

38. Page from the *Frankenstein* manuscripts, on which Mary Shelley has moved from a thick- to a fine-nibbed pen midway through a sentence.

the effect of that power. He constructed
a small electrical machine and exhibited a few experiments and made also a
kite with a wire and string which drew down
that fluid from the clouds.

This last stroke compleated
the overthrow of Cornelius Agrippa, Alber-
tus and Paracelsus, who had so long
reigned the lords of my imagination. But
by some fatality I did not feel inclined to
commence any modern system and this
disinclination was influenced by the following circumstance.

My father expressed a wish that I
should attend a course of lectures upon
natural Philosophy to which I consented cheerfully.
Some accident that I spent in town at the
house of Clerval's father I heard that
was at met Mr. — a professor
of chemistry who left the company at
an early hour

they are now stored, and stand as a reminder of the way in which the manuscripts, like Frankenstein's Creature, have been the object of dismemberment and reassemblage (fig. 37).

One of the features of the *Frankenstein* manuscripts to have received particular attention is the presence on its paper of marks made by two hands. Mary passed her draft to Shelley for editing and revision as she wrote, and his comments and emendations appear throughout Notebooks A and B. The physicality of the manuscript thus tells a story of cooperative creation, in which two voices are interspersed through the medium of ink on paper. The visual contrast between those voices is notable. Mary's hand travels across the pages of Notebook A in firm straight lines, in a brown ink that matches the tones of the paper. Occasionally the rhythm of her writing is interrupted by a blot, and three pages in she changes her pen for a thinner nib, resulting in strokes that are finer and fainter (fig. 38). The thick-nibbed pen makes the odd reappearance as the draft progresses, sometimes appearing mid-sentence in a manner that suggests she moved between pens as nibs failed. She deletes little as she writes, rarely crossing through more than a line at a time. When she does delete longer sections, she rewrites but keeps moving forward, rarely making repeated attempts at the same moment, and rarely trying out multiple constructions. Her hand is purposeful and clear-sighted and there is something remarkable about the clarity of her writing on the page. On fol. 22 recto of Notebook B, for example, the Creature's lament appears without hesitation, blot or correction to interrupt its complex modulations of syntax and reference (fig. 39). 'I remembered Adams supplication to his creator but where was mine? He had abbandoned [*sic*] me and in the bitterness of my heart I cursed him.'

contented & happy. Such were their few wishes. While I became every day more
miserable. increase of knowledge only clearly discovered to me more plainly what a wretched outcast I was. I cherished hope it is true but it vanished when I beheld my person reflected in the water or even my shadow in the moon-shine — I endeavoured to crush these fears and to fortify myself for the trial which in a few months I resolved to undergo; and sometimes I allowed my thoughts unchecked by reason to ramble in the fields of Paradise & dared to fancy amiable & lovely beings sympathizing with my feelings and cheering my gloom — their angelic countenances breathed smiles of consolation — But it was all a dream no Eve soothed my sorrows or shared my thoughts. I was alone. I remembered Adams supplication to his creator but where was mine? He had abbandoned me and in the bitterness of my heart I cursed him.

Autumn passed thus — with surprise & grief I saw the leaves decay & fall, & nature again assume the barren & bleak appearance it had when I first beheld the woods and the lovely moon. I did not heed the dreariness of the weather. By my constitution I was more fitted for the sufferance of cold than heat. But my only joys were

39. Page from the *Frankenstein* manuscripts with the Creature's lament.

Overlaid onto Mary's script throughout Notebooks A and B is Shelley's hand. Shelley wrote his annotations in a black ink that, in the Notebooks themselves (much less so in their facsimile and digital versions), stands in sharp contrast to the brown of Mary's pen. Shelley's script shifts in size according to where on the page he writes – sometimes between Mary's lines or over her words, sometimes in the margin. His pen, like hers, reveals its blots and moments of scratchiness. The width of his deletions varies throughout, appearing at points as a fine line through a word but at others a thick bar, suggesting a change of angle or pressure. His physicality is immanent in the manuscript in other ways: on fol. 11 verso and 12 recto of Notebook A, a pattern of symmetrical blots reveals him to have slammed the notebook shut while the ink was still wet (fig. 40). Still more overlaying of hands takes place at points where Shelley has written more substantial additions in the margins. On fol. 12 verso of Notebook A, Shelley has written an addition of several sentences in pencil in the margin, which Mary has then inked over as if to confirm the passage's inclusion in the text (fig. 41). The result is a draft that, for all its clarity of narrative and style, is arrestingly provisional. The deletions, ink splutters and two interwoven hands result in an artefact caught in the process of its own creation, the evolution of which is manifested in the physicality of the page. The manuscripts of *Frankenstein* thus stand as a physical representation of a work in progress: of conversations, of experiments in form, of a text revised and honed almost as fast as the hand holding the pen can move.

The substance of Shelley's additions and corrections has, over the years, been the subject of much critical debate. Scholars of different political persuasions have variously attributed much of the novel's power to his pen, or, in contrast, accused him of committing an act of patriarchal appropriation in seeking to impose his voice on his wife's work.[1] Other scholars have challenged such extreme readings, preferring instead to try to recreate an ongoing conversation between the Shelleys to which the *Frankenstein* manuscripts testify. One instance of this conversation takes place in Notebook A at the point on fol. 12 in which Mary has inked over a Shelley addition. Shelley's annotation comes in the conversation between Frankenstein and M. Waldman about the work of the alchemists:

> He said that these were men to whose indefatigable zeal modern philosophers were indebted for most of the foundations of their knowledge. They had left to us, as an easier task, to give new names, and arrange in connected classifications, the facts which they in a great degree had been the instruments of bringing to light. The labours of men of genius, however erroneously directed, scarcely ever fail in ultimately turning to the solid advantage of mankind.[2]

It would be easy to read this addition as a Shelleyan proclamation of the power of genius: a defence of solitary ambition in a novel that elsewhere is highly critical of the pursuit of knowledge for vainglorious ends. Yet his interpolation is more complicated than this. He certainly acknowledges the value of solitary ambition to the general good, but through Waldman's careful phrasing he emphasizes too that it is only within an intellectual community that genius has value. Waldman's conception of the duty of the scientist is fundamentally sociable and Shelley's addition insists on, rather than devalues, the novel's argument that social responsibility should be at the heart of scientific

of his ~~scheme~~. But when the no Besides I had a contempt for the uses
of modern ~~chemistry~~ natural philosophy. It was very
~~thin~~ different when these masters
of the science sought immortality
and ~~[power]~~; such views although
futile were grand; but now the scene was
all changed. ~~And the experim~~

the utmost
environ of
enquiries seemed
to limit itself
to the annihi-
lation of those
visions on which

My interest in science
was chiefly [bound]
I was required
to exchange
Chimeras of
boundless grandeur
for realities of
little worth.

~~of chimera~~ ~~overthrown~~ ~~at the same~~
~~time all greatness in the science~~
. Such were my reflections during
the two or three days, spent almost in ~~solitude~~
solitude: but at as the ensuing week
commenced I thought of the infor-
mation Mr Krempe had given me
concerning the lectures, and although
I could not consent to go and hear
that little conceited fellow deliver
sentences, out of a pulpit I recollected what he had
said of Mr Waldman, whom I had
never seen ~~and~~ as he had been
hitherto out of town.
Part~~ly~~ ~~of~~ curiosity ~~and~~ partly from
idleness I went into the lecturing room
which Mr Waldman entered shortly
after. This professor was a very different man from his colleague. He
was about fifty but with aspect expressive of the greatest benevolence
a few grey ~~hairs~~ hairs covered his temples

40. Pages from the *Frankenstein* manuscripts marked by symmetrical ink blots from Percy Shelley's pen.

but those at the back of his head were nearly black. He was short in person but remarkable erect and his voice the sweetest I had ever heard. He began his lecture with a *by a recapitulation of the* ~~history~~ of ~~his~~ history of chemistry and ~~several~~ the various improvements *made by various* men *of learning* ~~one may~~ pronouncing *with fervour* the names of the greatest discoverers ~~with great warmth~~. He then took a cursory view of the present state of ~~chemistry~~ *the science*, and explained many of its ~~terms~~ terms. *After making* a few preparatory experiments *he* concluded with a panegyric upon *modern* chemistry the words of which I shall never forget.

"The ancient teachers of this science said he," promised impossibilities "and performed nothing. The modern "masters promise very little. They "know that metals cannot be "transmuted and that the elixir *of life* is a chimaera. But "these philosophers whose ~~eyes~~ hands "appear only made to dabble in "dirt and their eyes to pore over "the microscope or crucible, "have indeed performed miracles. "They penetrate into the recesses of "nature and show how she works

"in her hiding places. They ascend into
"the heavens; they have discovered how
"the blood circulates, and the nature
"of the air we breathe. Nay they have
"acquired new and almost unlimi
"ted powers, — They can command the
"thunders of heaven, mimick the
"earthquake, and even mock the
"invisible world with its own
"shadows."

I departed highly pleased with
the professor and his lecture &
paid him a visit the same evening.
His manners in private were even
more mild & attractive than in public. For
there was a certain dignity in his
manner during his lectures which
was replaced by the greatest affability
affability and kindness in his own
house. He heard my little narration
concerning my studies with attention
smiled at the names of Cornelius
Agrippa and Paracelsus but without
the contempt that Mr Krempe had
& exhibited. ~~I ended by saying~~ that
his lecture had removed my prejudice
against modern chemists and request-
ed at the same time his advice
concerning the books I ought to procure

He said that
these were
men to whose
indefatigable zeal
modern
philosophers were
indebted for most
of the foundation
of their knowledge
~~and had~~
~~the~~ They left to
us, as an easier
task to give new
names & arrange
in conected clasi-
fications the
facts which they
to a great degree
have been the
instruments of
bringing to light
The labours of
men of genius
however erroneously
directed scarce-
ly ever failed.

41. Page from the *Frankenstein* manuscripts with a pencilled addition by Percy Shelley in the margin, later inked over by Mary Shelley. The pencilling is just visible underneath the ink.

pursuit. Elsewhere Shelley highlights the naivety of Frankenstein's enthusiasm for the alchemists, and the all-encompassing nature of his delusions. 'I was required to exchange chimeras of boundless grandeur', he has Frankenstein say, 'for realities of little worth.'[3] Frankenstein is culpable, Mary's narrative tells us, precisely because of his pursuit of 'chimeras of boundless grandeur' and because of his rejection of socially responsible scientific ambition. Shelley's language ('grandeur', 'little worth') points towards the vanity of Frankenstein's attachment to visions of glory, and suggests he perceives modern science as a violent annihilator of his dreams. Here and elsewhere, Shelley's additions and revisions work in concert with Mary's work, suggesting that he served above all as a good editor, concerned with drawing out the novel's thematic grace notes rather than with imposing a competing vision of creativity onto his wife's work.

The *Frankenstein* manuscripts reflect the physiognomic theories of Johann Caspar Lavater, the Swiss thinker whose account of the way in which the characters of individuals could be read by studying their physical features was enormously influential in the late eighteenth and early nineteenth centuries. The Shelleys probably knew Lavater's work through Thomas Holcroft's translation of *Essays on Physiognomy* (1793), and through the championing of Henry Fuseli, Lavater's old friend and most vocal supporter in England. Lavater describes physiognomy as a process of decoding internal characteristics by reading external appearances, and he argues that the complexities of life can be better understood through the application of his method. 'Is not', he asks, 'all nature physiognomy, superficies and contents, body and spirit, exterior effect and internal power, invisible beginning and visible ending?'[4] Frankenstein's Creature is a victim of this kind of analysis, and Frankenstein is guilty of judging his creation's soul according to its physical representation. Frankenstein is guilty, too, of a further physiognomic failure: he has made a being from parts selected on the basis of their beauty, but whose exterior reveals its internal anatomical workings and who thus has no surface to be read.

Both the Shelleys invested handwriting and other physical signs of the body on the page with a great deal of significance. Scholars of Mary's life and work have repeatedly noted that her handwriting became increasingly like Shelley's over the course of her marriage.[5] After Shelley's death Mary used her immersion in his manuscripts to enact a dialogue with him in the pages of her private journal. 'What a scene to recur to,' she wrote as she read through old letters in October 1822. 'My William, Clara, Allegra are all talked of – They lived then – They breathed this air & their voices struck on my sense, their feet trod the earth beside me – & their hands were warm with blood & life when clasped in mine.'[6] Mary kept Shelley's letters and manuscripts by her for the rest of her life, stowing the most precious documents in a travelling desk that rarely left her side. Body and paper became one in her desk, where she also kept an organ she believed to be Shelley's heart, wrapped in leaves from a copy of his poem *Adonais*. Shelley, meanwhile, believed firmly that handwriting was expressive of character, and that ink on paper offered the possibility of a graphical manifestation of the mind. 'The handwriting of Ariosto', he told his friend Thomas Love Peacock, 'is a small firm and pointed character expressing as I should say a strong but keen circumscribed energy of mind, that of Tasso is

42. Page from the association copy of *Adonais*, 1821. Mary used leaves from her copy of this book to wrap Shelley's heart.

LI.

Here pause: these graves are all too young as yet
To have out grown the sorrow which consigned
Its charge to each; and if the seal is set,
Here, on one fountain of a mourning mind,
Break it not thou! too surely shalt thou find
Thine own well full, if thou returnest home,
Of tears and gall. From the world's bitter wind
Seek shelter in the shadow of the tomb.
What Adonais is, why fear we to become?

LII.

The One remains, the many change and pass;
Heaven's light forever shines, Earth's shadows fly;
Life, like a dome of many-coloured glass,
Stains the white radiance of Eternity,
Until Death tramples it to fragments. — Die,
If thou wouldst be with that which thou dost seek!
Follow where all is fled! — Rome's azure sky,
Flowers, ruins, statues, music, words, are weak
The glory they transfuse with fitting truth to speak.

LIII.

Why linger, why turn back, why shrink, my Heart?
Thy hopes are gone before: from all things here
They have departed; thou shouldst now depart!
A light is past from the revolving year,
And man, and woman; and what still is dear
Attracts to crush, repels to make thee wither.
The soft sky smiles,——the low wind whispers near:
'Tis Adonais calls! oh, hasten thither,
No more let Life divide what Death can join together.

large free and flowing except there is a checked expression in the midst of the flow which brings the letters into a smaller compass than one expected from the beginning of the word.' 'You know', he continued, 'I always seek in what I see the manifestation of something beyond the present and tangible object.'[7]

Shelley's method of reading character through handwriting is clearly indebted to Lavater, and offers a way of reading the *Frankenstein* manuscripts as animate objects in which conversation and collaboration are captured by the physical signs on a page passed between two hands. The novel itself offers an alternative parable, in which imaginative delusions inspired by Lavater lead to dangerous misreadings of the body. Frankenstein believes that he can discover 'the tremendous secrets of the human frame' through grave-robbing and dissection.[8] His knowledge of the anatomy of the dead does indeed enable him to discover the animating spark of life, but he remains ignorant of the depths beyond bones and muscle. His Creature is never able to be fully human because Frankenstein fails to understand the centrality of the soul in the dead bodies he studies. The Creature is thus simultaneously a result of an overactive imagination and a consequently perverted reading of the materials of life: the result too of a failure of imaginative sympathy with the human beings whose form Frankenstein tries to mimic. The Creature's narrative makes it clear that his character has been formed by his reading, rather than by his physical components. His body has no influence on his character, other than to enrage him as he realizes the extent to which his hideous countenance excludes him from human society.

Lavater's work thus illustrates the links between *Frankenstein*'s story (which is at once a critique of physiognomy and an acknowledgement of its power) and its composition. The co-created manuscript is a physiognomic artefact, and has been read as such by literary scholars determined to reanimate the Shelleys' conversation by studying the marks made by hands and ink. Such readings are seductive and need to be treated with caution, but Mary and Shelley do both appear in the manuscripts of *Frankenstein* through their handwriting. As a result the manuscripts comprise a body of work in which a narrative of sociable creation is revealed and which in its turn stands as an alternative to the model of egotistical creativity depicted in the novel itself. Mary's draft, read in concert with Shelley's annotations, enacts a drama of composition, producing a physiognomic text in two hands in which conversation leaves a bodily trace on paper.

Conflations of *Frankenstein* as a bodily text and the body of the creature have characterized writing on the novel since its publication. The first edition was published at the beginning of 1818 (fig. 43), and in January the *Quarterly Review* characterized it as 'a tissue of horrible and disgusting absurdity'.[9] Most of the early reviewers were similarly damning, although Walter Scott proved an exception to this, writing in *Blackwood's Edinburgh Magazine* of his delight at the novel's imaginative power. The novel was published anonymously but Scott thought that its author revealed, if not their name, then 'uncommon powers of poetic imagination', and his conclusion was a model of literary generosity: 'If Gray's definition of Paradise, to lie on a couch, namely, and read new novels, come any thing near truth, no small praise is due to him, who, like the author of Frankenstein, has enlarged the sphere of that fascinating enjoyment.'[10] Scott also surmised Shelley to be the author of *Frankenstein*: a deduction based on the novel's dedication to Godwin and its similarities to Godwin's novel *St. Leon*. When Mary wrote to Scott to thank him for his review she was quick to correct his misapprehension. 'I am anxious', she wrote, 'to prevent your continuing in the mistake of supposing Mr Shelley guilty of a juvenile attempt of mine; to which – from its being written at an early age, I abstained from putting my name.'[11] Her excuse for writing to Scott – to clear Shelley of the imputation of authorship – should perhaps not be taken literally. Instead, Mary's letter reads as the statement of an author finally taking back the pages of her manuscript, and claiming them as her own.

43. First edition of *Frankenstein*, 1818.

FRANKENSTEIN;

OR,

THE MODERN PROMETHEUS.

IN THREE VOLUMES.

Did I request thee, Maker, from my clay
To mould me man? Did I solicit thee
From darkness to promote me?——
PARADISE LOST.

VOL. I.

London:
PRINTED FOR
LACKINGTON, HUGHES, HARDING, MAVOR, & JONES,
FINSBURY SQUARE.

1818.

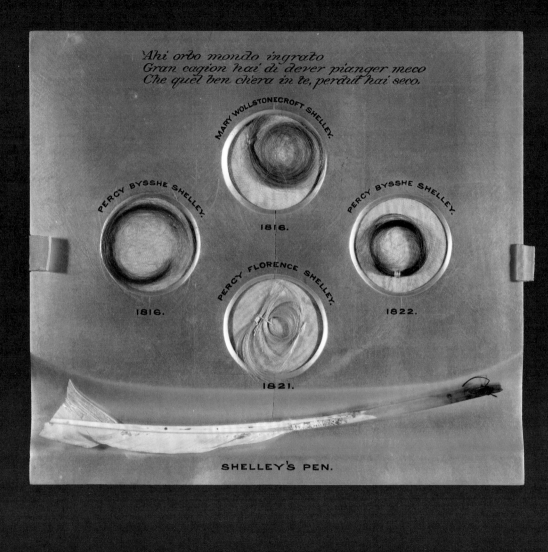

Ahi orbo mondo ingrato
Gran cagion hai di dever pianger meco
Che quel ben ch'era in te, perdut hai seco.

MARY WOLLSTONECROFT SHELLEY.

PERCY BYSSHE SHELLEY.

PERCY BYSSHE SHELLEY.

1816.

PERCY FLORENCE SHELLEY.

1816.

1822.

1821.

SHELLEY'S PEN.

5
RELICS

'Are we creating a new Frankenstein?' asked a senior employee of the World Economic Forum in March 2017. Writing for *Forbes Magazine*, Paolo Gallo argued that *Frankenstein* offered a productive metaphor for those gathered in Davos to think through the potential of emerging technologies. 'We cannot delegate ethical choices and our moral responsibilities to algorithms,' he wrote. 'We cannot think that computers give us the opportunity to escape from our responsibilities, our choices, our freedom.' And yet, he concluded, 'if we use our contextual intelligence to connect Frankenstein, Industrial Revolutions, Artificial Intelligence and our own moral compass, we will realize that, as artists, we shall write, paint, sculpt and play out our own choices.'[1] In the same month, the Canadian Ambassador to the United States slammed the Trump administration's proposed border tariff, calling it a 'half-consumption-tax', a 'Frankenstein V.A.T.'.[2]

Critical opinion is divided about the origins of Frankenstein's name. Some scholars point to Frankenstein Castle in Germany as its

44. Framed locks of hair belonging to Mary and Percy Shelley and their son Percy Florence.

source; others to François-Félix Nogaret's 1790 poetic allegory *Le Miroir*, which features an inventor of automated figures who rejoices in the unlikely name of Wak-wik-vauk-on-son-frankénsteïn. Not in doubt is that within a few years of the publication of Mary's novel, the name had entered the language as a catch-all political metaphor, capable of all manner of rhetorical reconfigurations. Speaking in the House of Commons in 1824, the Foreign Secretary George Canning positioned *Frankenstein* as a cautionary tale in support of his advocacy for the policy of amelioration (as opposed to immediate abolition) in a debate about the future of slavery in the British Empire. Canning favoured a gradualist approach to emancipation, arguing that to free a slave 'in the manhood of his physical strength, in the maturity of his physical passions, but in the infancy of his uninstructed reason, would be to raise up a creature resembling the splendid fiction of a recent romance; the hero of which constructs a human form, with all the corporeal capabilities of man, and with the thews and sinews of a giant; but being unable to impart to the work of his hands a perception of right and wrong, he finds too late that he has only created a more than mortal power of doing mischief, and himself recoils from the monster which he has made.'[3] Canning was the first in a long line of political actors and commentators to read *Frankenstein* as a morality tale on the dangers of innovation and sudden change. This was how the novel was figured in political cartoons of the mid-nineteenth century: in 1843 *Punch* carried an image of a monstrous Irishman attacking a diminutive British bystander under the caption 'The Irish Frankenstein'. The Creature's giant-like physical status was emphasized in early illustrated editions of the novel (fig. 45) and was the characteristic on which John Tenniel focused in his 1882 cartoon for *Punch* in which

45. Frontispiece of the third edition of *Frankenstein*, 1831, with an early illustration of the Creature.

the comparison between the Irish leader Charles Stewart Parnell and *Frankenstein*'s Creature is accentuated through quotation from Mary's text (fig. 46). During the Cold War *Frankenstein* served as a potent symbol of the fears of a world on the brink of nuclear war: 'for all we know', pronounced a radio broadcaster on the day of the Hiroshima blast, 'we have created a Frankenstein'.[4] In the first decades of the twenty-first century, meanwhile, opponents of genetically modified crops reached for variants of the label 'Frankenstein food' to encapsulate an interconnected set of arguments about scientific experimentation, profit and risk.[5]

Frankenstein has thus been refashioned, in the two centuries since its publication, for the purposes of both the left and the right, until it has become a proxy through which Western culture articulates the anxieties of an age. 'If the worst enemies of conservatism were to construct a Frankenstein figure that represents the worst elements of right-wing politics,' proclaimed the *Washington Post* in 2016, 'Donald Trump would be it.'[6] 'The EU is a Frankenstein's monster, doomed to fail,' screamed a headline on the online *UKIPDaily* a year later.[7] It is a critical commonplace to say that novels take on a life of their own after publication but *Frankenstein* lives on in metaphor like no other, anatomized and dissected according to the preoccupations of each generation, and today it continues to produce a series of images to frame conversations about a world in which technological innovation at times appears to outstrip human control.

Part of the explanation for the cultural power of *Frankenstein* lies in the fact that in the two hundred years since its first publication it has given rise to a number of highly visual iterations of itself. In the twentieth century the great institutions of Hollywood made the story

THE IRISH FRANKENSTEIN.

"The baneful and blood-stained Monster * * * yet was it not my Master to the very extent that it was my Creature ? * * * Had I not breathed into it my own spirit ?" * * * (*Extract from the Works of* C. S. P-RN-LL, M.P.)

46. Tenniel, 'The Irish Frankenstein', from *Punch*, 1882.

47. Boris Karloff as Frankenstein's monster, from the 1931 Universal Pictures film.

their own, and for many the Creature of popular imagination today still remains the bolt-necked anti-hero immortalized by Boris Karloff in the 1931 Universal Pictures film. Karloff-inspired Frankensteins have appeared in recent years on the British stage in an acclaimed production at the National Theatre, and in a much-criticized adaptation by the Royal Ballet. *Frankenstein* has been the subject of affectionate parody as well as adaptation: Tim Burton's *Frankenweenie* is notable for the way it pokes fun at both the novel and its cinematic offspring. The first visual reworking of Mary's text took place on the stage of London's Lyceum Theatre in 1823, to the horror of London's moral guardians. The *Theatrical Observer* of 9 August 1823 reported that placards had appeared throughout the city with a warning to 'The Play-Going Public':

> Do not go to the Lyceum to see the monstrous Drama, founded on the improper work called 'Frankenstein' – Do not take your wives and families ... This subject is pregnant with mischief.[8]

Mary's biographer Miranda Seymour suggests that these placards may well have been manufactured by the Lyceum management in order to drum up public excitement about the production, and when Mary returned to England in 1823 the stage production's success meant that she attracted attention.[9] 'She looks elegant and sickly and young,' noted the diarist Henry Crabb Robinson. 'One would not suppose that she was the author of "Frankenstein".'[10]

Mary herself rather approved of the Lyceum's production, which she saw a few days after her return. 'Lo & behold!', she wrote to a friend, 'I found myself famous!':

Frankenstein had prodigious success as a drama & was about to be repeated for the 23rd night at the English opera house. The play bill amused me extremely, for in the list of dramatis personae came, — by Mr T. Cooke: this nameless mode of naming the un[n]ameable is rather good. On Friday Aug. 29th Jane My father William & I went to the theatre to see it. Wallack looked very well as F - he is at the beginning full of hope & expectation - at the end of the Ist Act. the stage represents a room with a staircase leading to F workshop - he goes to it and you see his light at a small window, through which a frightened servant peeps, who runs off in terror when F. exclaims "It lives!" - Presently F himself rushes in horror & trepidation from the room and while still expressing his agony & terror — throws down the door of the labratory, [sic] leaps the staircase & presents his unearthly & monstrous person on the stage. ... I was much amused, & it appeared to excite a breathelss [sic] eagerness in the audience.[11]

Mary's father William Godwin arranged for the novel to be reprinted in order to capitalize on the interest generated by the 1823 production, and revised adaptations continued to be staged in London and Paris throughout the 1820s. Mary's 1831 reworking of the novel, meanwhile, illustrated via its internal alterations and accompanying Introduction that the text of *Frankenstein* also remained dynamic and unstable, and that the story of its creation was a subject of fascination for even its earliest readers.

Mary's own story in the years following the publication of *Frankenstein* in 1818 was dominated by a series of tragedies. A few months after the novel appeared her baby daughter Clara died of dysentery contracted

48. Benedict Cumberbatch and Jonny Lee Miller in the National Theatre's 2011 production of *Frankenstein*, directed by Danny Boyle.

49. Playbill for *Presumption: or the Fate of Frankenstein*, the theatrical adaptation that Mary saw on her return to England in 1823.

during a long hot journey across Italy. Less than a year later her son William, now aged three, contracted malaria and died in Rome. Mary was broken by her double loss, and in the months following William's death sank into deep depression. 'My dearest Mary, wherefore hast thou gone/ And left me in this dreary world alone?', wrote Shelley that summer:

> Thy form is here indeed, a lovely one;
> But thou art fled, gone down the dreary road
> Which leads to sorrows most obscure abode;
> Thou sittest on the heath of pale despair;
>   Where
> For thine own sake I cannot follow thee.[12]

Mary's mood lifted following the birth of her fourth child Percy Florence in 1819 – the only one of her children to survive into adulthood. Yet she remained serious and reserved, very unlike the tartan-clad adventurer of her girlhood. She resumed writing, producing a meditation on grief and incestuous love that remained unpublished in her lifetime, and then a second full-length novel, set during the period of the Italian Renaissance. In 1822 the Shelleys moved from Pisa to the Casa Magni on the Gulf of Spezia, where they planned to spend the summer. There Mary suffered a miscarriage that nearly killed her, and from there Shelley departed in his boat to greet friends who had arrived from England. On his way back he was caught in a storm and drowned.

Mary was twenty-four when Shelley died. The heightened drama of the eight years between 1814 and 1822 – years in which she wrote *Frankenstein*, lived with Shelley and bore and lost her children – would

50. Louis Fournier, *The Funeral of Shelley*, 1889. Fournier depicts Mary kneeling to one side of Shelley's funeral pyre but in reality she remained in Pisa while male friends orchestrated and attended his cremation.

51. A page from Mary Shelley's 'Journal of Sorrow', dating from October 1822. 'I have now no friend,' she writes.

shape the rest of her life. Shelley was cremated on the beach at Viareggio, in a ceremony somewhat inaccurately portrayed by Louis Fournier many decades later (fig. 50). Mary moved with her infant son to Genoa, where she kept a diary she called her 'Journal of Sorrow' (fig. 51). 'When I meditate or dream on my future life, one idea alone animates me,' ran one entry. 'I think of friends & human intercourse ... [and] I weep to think how unstable all that is.'[13] When she returned

October 2 1822. Genoa September ___ ___

On the eighth of July I finished my journal. This
is a curious coincidence: — The date still remains, the
fatal 8th — a monument to shew that all ended
then. And I begin again? — oh never! But several
motives induce me, when the day has gone down,
and all is silent around me, steeped in sleep, to pen,
as occasion wills, my reflexions & feelings. First, I
have now no friend. For eight years ~~I~~ I
communicated with unlimited freedom with one whose genius, far transcending mine, awakened & guided my
thoughts; I conversed with him; rectified my errors of
judgement, obtained new lights from him, & my
mind was satisfied. Now I am alone! Oh, how
alone! The stars may behold my tears, & the
winds drink my sighs — but my thoughts are
a sealed treasure which I can confide to none.
White paper — wilt thou be my confident?

to England in 1823 it was with two purposes in mind. Her first priority was to earn enough money to support herself and Percy Florence and in order to do so she turned hack writer, producing reams of words for journals and periodicals, and four further novels. Her second ambition was to curate Shelley's legacy for an unappreciative world, both by making his poetry available and by telling his story. Her first edition of Shelley's poetry, *Posthumous Poems*, was published in 1824 and almost immediately suppressed by Shelley's irate father, who had no wish to see his aberrant son's name brought before the public. It took Mary years to wear down Sir Timothy Shelley's opposition to publication, and by the late 1830s she was still only able to publish a biography of Shelley by presenting it as extended notes to his poems. Nevertheless, thanks to her efforts Shelley's name was gradually rehabilitated as new generations of readers – among them young poets such as Browning and Tennyson – paid more attention to his poetry than to old stories about atheism and scandalous living.

52. Shelley's watch and their seals, which Mary kept for the rest of her life.

Mary was not content, however, to nourish Shelley's memory only in public. She kept any object with which Shelley had a bodily association – his watch, his glove, a lock of his hair – along with physical mementos of her parents and her son. In 1848 she was joined by a new custodian of the Shelley flame, following Percy Florence's marriage to Jane Gibson St John. Jane was passionately devoted to her mother-in-law and much more interested in her husband's distinguished intellectual ancestry than he. She created a shrine to Shelley and Mary at her house in Dorset, and proved herself in the second half of the nineteenth century to be a doughty defender of their names. Mary died of a brain tumour in 1851, when she was fifty-three. Her final years were made happy by Jane and Percy Florence, but she never lost the sensation of having outlived her generation. 'The happiness I enjoyed and the suffering I endured in Italy make present pleasures & annoyances appear like the changes of a mask,' she wrote in 1824. 'I can sometimes for a while enter into the spirit of the game, but my affections are in the past & my imagination is not much exalted by a representation mean & puerile when compared to the real delight of my intercourse [with] my exalted Shelley ... and others then of less note, but remembered now with fon[dness] as having made a part of the Elect.'[14]

Frankenstein remained at the heart of Mary's own contested legacy long after her death. The writer of the one substantial obituary to appear thought that the novel would ensure her 'a peculiar place among the gifted women of England',[15] yet the vicar at Boscombe Church in Dorset refused to accept her body for burial. Jane Shelley, who had organized the exhumation of the coffins of Godwin and Wollstonecraft from their London burial plots in order to lay them next to their daughter, sat outside the churchyard with all three coffins

53. Lady Shelley. The wistful look captured here belies Jane's steely control of the Shelleys' legacy.

until he relented. In 1975 plans to erect a blue plaque outside the house in which Mary lived in London were thwarted by the occupier objecting to having his house defaced with the word 'Frankenstein'. 'I'm not keen to have the phrase "author of Frankenstein" emblazoned across the plaque, especially as the house is a vicarage,' he complained to the Greater London Council. 'I would rather that it were re-worded to read

54. Percy Florence Shelley.

"author(ess) and wife of the poet".'[16] Mary finally got her blue plaque in 2003, complete with wording acceptable to the feminist scholars who have played a crucial role over the past fifty years in establishing her centrality to the literary canon. The plaque remains in place today and reads simply 'Mary Shelley, 1797–1851, author of Frankenstein. Lived here 1846–1851.'

TO THE MEMORY OF
PERCY BYSSHE SHELLEY,
POET,
BORN AT FIELD PLACE IN THE COUNTY OF SUSSEX, AUGUST 4, 1792,
DROWNED BY THE UPSETTING OF HIS BOAT IN THE GULF OF SPEZZIA JULY, 1822;
HIS ASHES ARE INTERRED IN THE PROTESTANT BURIAL GROUND AT ROME.

ALSO TO THE MEMORY OF
MARY WOLLSTONECRAFT SHELLEY, HIS WIFE,
BORN AUGUST 30, 1797, DIED FEBRUARY 1, 1851,
HER REMAINS ARE INTERRED, TOGETHER WITH THOSE OF HER FATHER WILLIAM GODWIN,
AND HER MOTHER MARY WOLLSTONECRAFT GODWIN,
IN THE CHURCHYARD AT BOURNEMOUTH.

"HE HAS OUT-SOARED THE SHADOW OF OUR NIGHT;
ENVY AND CALUMNY, AND HATE AND PAIN,
AND THAT UNREST WHICH MEN MISCALL DELIGHT,
CAN TOUCH HIM NOT AND TORTURE NOT AGAIN;
FROM THE CONTAGION OF THE WORLD'S SLOW STAIN
HE IS SECURE, AND NOW CAN NEVER MOURN
A HEART GROWN COLD, A HEAD GROWN GREY IN VAIN;
NOR WHEN THE SPIRIT'S SELF HAS CEASED TO BURN,
WITH SPARKLESS ASHES LOAD AN UNLAMENTED URN."

SHELLEY'S ADONAIS.

Relics are animated in *Frankenstein*, given new life by a young man of huge ambition and imagination whose tragedy is to forget his responsibilities to the people around him in pursuit of his dreams. The novel is itself a work of assemblage, in which an interconnected collection of ideas, influences, objects, people and papers are brought together in a particular set of places. *Frankenstein* lives on because of the circumstances of its creation, and because its influences remain visible. It is an uneven novel written by a young woman deeply engaged in the process of working out what she thinks about the world: about science, politics, religion, slavery, maternity, the imagination, creativity and community. The result is a taut, brilliant synthesis of preoccupations and developing ideas. To readers similarly preoccupied by the question of how to understand the world around them, therefore, its imaginative potential is endless. From Mary Shelley's imagination grew a creature made not of limbs but of ideas: ideas which take us back into the world of their origins, and forward into our own historical moment. I began with her anarchic image of invention emerging 'not out of void, but out of chaos'.[17] This messy, rich and unpredictable conception of the inventive mind remains as potent and exciting now as it was two hundred years ago. *Frankenstein* will continue to endure just as long as humans have the capacity to imagine impossible futures, and then to be frightened by the consequences of their imagination.

55. Henry Weekes, Shelley Memorial at Priory Church, Christchurch, Dorset, depicting Mary as Pietà, cradling Shelley's body in her arms.

NOTES

Preface

1   M. Shelley, 'Introduction', *Frankenstein; or The Modern Prometheus* (1831), ed. M.K. Joseph, Oxford, Oxford University Press, 1969, p. 8.

2   M. Shelley, *Frankenstein; or The Modern Prometheus* (1818), ed. M. Butler, Oxford, Oxford University Press, 1993, p. 34.

3   Shelley, *Frankenstein* (1831), 'Introduction', p. 10.

1. Time

1   The question of names is a tricky one when writing about the Shelleys, and most biographers default to calling Percy Bysshe Shelley 'Shelley' and Mary Shelley 'Mary'. This follows the pattern that they and their friends adopted, and is one I will adopt here.

2   Shelley, *Frankenstein* (1831), 'Introduction', p. 8.

3   Shelley, *Frankenstein* (1831), 'Introduction', pp. 9–10.

4   Preface to 'Kubla Kahn' in S.T. Coleridge, *The Major Works*, ed. H.J. Jackson, Oxford, Oxford University Press, 1985, p. 102.

5   'Preface to *Lyrical Ballads*' (1802), in W. Wordsworth, *The Major Works*, ed. S. Gill, Oxford, Oxford University Press, 1984, p. 597.

6   Shelley, *Frankenstein* (1831), 'Introduction', p. 7.

7   Shelley, *Frankenstein* (1831), 'Introduction', pp. 7–8.

8   W.M. Rossetti (ed.), *The Diary of Dr John William Polidori, 1816, Relating to Byron, Shelley, etc.* London, Elkin Matthews, 1911, p. 128.

9   Shelley, *Frankenstein* (1818), p. 39.

10   Shelley, *Frankenstein* (1831), 'Introduction', pp. 8–9.

11   E. Darwin, *The Temple of Nature*, London, Joseph Johnson, 1806, p. 197.

12   Darwin, *Temple*, p. 201.

13   M. Butler, 'Introduction', *Frankenstein* (1818), p. xxxiv.

14   J.W. Croker, review of *Frankenstein*, *Quarterly Review* (January 1818), pp. 379–85, at p. 381.

15   Shelley, *Frankenstein* (1818), p. 184.

2. People

1   S.T. Coleridge to R. Southey, 24/12/1799 in S.T. Coleridge, *Collected Letters*, ed. E.L. Griggs, Oxford, Clarendon Press, 2000, I, p. 305.

2   Shelley, *Frankenstein* (1831), 'Introduction', p. 5.

3   Shelley, *Frankenstein* (1831), 'Introduction', p. 6.

4 Charles Clairmont to Claire
   Clairmont, 13-20/09/1815, in
   M.K. Stocking (ed.), *The Clairmont
   Correspondence*, 2 vols, Baltimore, MD,
   Johns Hopkins University Press, I,
   pp. 14–15.
5 Claire Clairmont to Lord Byron,
   March/April 1816, in *The Clairmont
   Correspondence*, I, p. 24.
6 P. Feldman and D. Scott-Kilvert,
   (eds), *The Journals of Mary Shelley,
   1814–1844*, 2 vols, Oxford, Clarendon
   Press, 1987, II, p. 439.
7 T. Medwin, *Conversations of Lord Byron*,
   ed. E.J. Lovell Jr, Princeton, NJ,
   Princeton University Press, 1966,
   p. 53.
8 Rossetti, *William Polidori*, p. 121.
9 Feldman and Scott-Kilvert, *Journals of
   Mary Shelley*, I, p. 127.
10 F. Imlay suicide note, 03/10/1816,
   in Stocking (ed.), *The Clairmont
   Correspondence*, I, p. 73.
11 Shelley, *Frankenstein* (1818), p. 78.
12 H. Shelley suicide note, ?07/12/1816,
   in D. Reiman et al., *Shelley and his
   Circle*, 10 vols to date, Cambridge,
   MA, Harvard University Press, 1961–,
   IV, pp. 805–6.
13 Shelley, *Frankenstein* (1818), p. 97.
14 Shelley, *Frankenstein* (1818), p. 77.
15 Shelley, *Frankenstein* (1818), p. 190.

3. Place

1 M. Shelley to F. Imlay, 01/06/1816, in
   B.T. Bennett (ed.), *The Letters of Mary
   Wollstonecraft Shelley*, 3 vols, Baltimore,
   MD, Johns Hopkins University Press,
   1980–8, I, p. 20.
2 Shelley, *Frankenstein* (1818), p. 24.
3 M. Shelley to M. Gisborne,
   15/08/1822, in Bennett (ed.), *The Letters
   of Mary Shelley*, I, p. 244.
4 Shelley, *Frankenstein* (1818), p. 191.
5 P. Feldman and D. Scott-Kilvert,
   (eds), *Journals of Mary Shelley*, I, p. 119.
6 Shelley, *Frankenstein* (1818), p. 76.
7 P. Shelley, *Poetry and Prose*, ed. D.
   Reiman and Neil Fraistat, New York,
   W.W. Norton and Company, 2002,
   p. 101.
8 M. Shelley to P. Shelley, 05/12/1816, in
   Bennett (ed.), *The Letters of Mary Shelley*,
   I, p. 22.
9 Shelley, *Frankenstein* (1818), pp. 136–7.
10 Shelley, *Frankenstein* (1818), p. 118.

4. Paper

1 See, for example, J. Rieger,
   'Introduction', in Mary
   Wollstonecraft Shelley, *Frankenstein*,
   (1831) pp. xi–xxvii; and, for an
   alternative perspective, Anne K.
   Mellor, *Mary Shelley: Her Life, Her Fiction,*

Her Monsters, London, Routledge, 1988, passim.

2 Shelley, *Frankenstein* (1818), p. 31.

3 Shelley, *Frankenstein* (1818), p. 30. Shelley's addition at Notebook A, fol. 11v.

4 Johann Caspar Lavater, *Essays on Physiognomy*, trans. T. Holcroft, London, G.G.J. and J. Robinson, 1793, p. 31.

5 See, for example B.T. Bennett, writing in *Romantic Revisions*: 'Just after she eloped with Shelley, her handwriting was distinct for the squared nature of the individual characters, but during the couple's years together her handwriting came to strongly resemble his.' Bennett, 'Finding Mary Shelley in Her Letters', in *Romantic Revisions*, ed. R. Brinkley and K. Hanley, Cambridge, Cambridge University Press, 1992, pp. 291–306, at p. 296.

6 P. Feldman and D. Scott-Kilvert, (eds), *Journals of Mary Shelley*, II, p. 435.

7 P. Shelley to T. Peacock, 07/11/1818, in F.L. Jones (ed.), *The Letters of Percy Bysshe Shelley*, 2 vols, Oxford, Clarendon Press, 1964, II, p. 47.

8 Shelley, *Frankenstein* (1818), p. 36.

9 Croker, review of *Frankenstein*, p. 382.

10 W. Scott, review of *Frankenstein*, *Blackwood's Edinburgh Magazine*, 2 March 1818, pp. 613–20, at p. 620.

11 MWS to W. Scott, 14/06/1818, in Bennett (ed.), *The Letters of Mary Shelley*, I, p. 71.

5. Relics

1 P. Gallo, 'Are We Creating a New Frankenstein?', https://www.forbes.com/sites/worldeconomicforum/2017/03/17/are-we-creating-a-new-frankenstein/#5b1fad373dc2 (accessed 21 March 2017).

2 J. Wingrove and A. Mayeda, '"Frankenstein" U.S. Border Tax Will Hurt Consumers, Canada Warns', *Bloomberg Politics*, 03/03/2017. https://www.bloomberg.com/politics/articles/2017-03-03/-frankenstein-u-s-border-tax-will-hurt-consumers-canada-warns (accessed 21 March 2017).

3 George Canning, 'Amelioration of the Condition of the Slave Population in the West Indies', House of Commons, 16/03/1824. *Hansard* HC Deb 16 March 1824 vol. 10 cc 1091–198. http://hansard.millbanksystems.com/commons/1824/mar/16/amelioration-of-the-condition-of-

the#S2Voo10Po_18240316_HOC_61 (accessed 21 March /2017).

4   Quoted in D. Ropeik, 'The Rise of Nuclear-Fear – How We Learned to Fear the Radiation', *Scientific American Online*, 15/06/2012. https://blogs.scientificamerican.com/guest-blog/the-rise-of-nuclear-fear-how-we-learned-to-fear-the-bomb/ (accessed 21 March 2017).

5   Examples of this abound in news archives from the late 1990s to the present day. See, for example, http://www.huffingtonpost.com/ellen-kanner/meatless-monday-gmos-a-fr_b_2008873.html (accessed 21 March 2017).

6   https://www.washingtonpost.com/opinions/the-gops-monster/2016/03/31/713cac6e-f771-11e5-a3ce-f06b5ba21f33_story.html?utm_term=.8bf98b269750 (accessed 21 March 2017).

7   http://www.ukipdaily.com/eu-is-a-frankenstein/ (accessed 21 March 2017).

8   *Theatrical Observer*, 9 August 1823, quoted in M. Seymour, *Mary Shelley*, London, John Murray, 2000, p. 334.

9   See Seymour, *Mary Shelley*, p. 334.

10 T. Sadler, ed., *Diary, Reminiscences and Correspondence of Henry Crabb Robinson*, 3 vols, London, Macmillan and Co., 1869, II, p. 260.

11 M. Shelley to L. Hunt, 11/09/1823, in Bennett (ed.), *The Letters of Mary Shelley*, I, p. 378.

12 I. Massey (ed.), *Posthumous Poems of Shelley: Mary Shelley's Fair Copy Book*, Montreal, McGill-Queens University Press, 1969, p. 88.

13 P. Feldman and D. Scott-Kilvert (eds), *The Journals of Mary Shelley*, II, p. 430.

14 M. Shelley to T.J. Hogg, 03/10/1824, in Bennett (ed.), *The Letters of Mary Shelley*, I, p. 450.

15 *Athenaeum*, 15/02/1851, quoted in Seymour, *Mary Shelley*, p. 539.

16 J. Morrison, 'Mary Shelley to get blue plaque at last', *The Independent*, 13/09/2003.

17 Shelley, *Frankenstein* (1818), 'Introduction', p. 8.

FURTHER READING

PRIMARY SOURCES

Bennett, B.T. (ed.), *The Letters of Mary Wollstonecraft Shelley*, 3 vols, Baltimore, MD, Johns Hopkins University Press, 1980–8.

Coleridge, S.T., *The Major Works*, ed. H.J. Jackson, Oxford, Oxford University Press, 1985.

Croker, J.W., review of *Frankenstein*, *Quarterly Review*, January 1818, pp. 379–85.

Darwin, Erasmus, *The Temple of Nature*, London, Joseph Johnson, 1806.

Feldman, P. and D. Scott-Kilvert (eds), *The Journals of Mary Shelley, 1814–1844*, 2 vols, Oxford, Clarendon Press, 1987.

Griggs, E.L. (ed.), *Collected Letters of Samuel Taylor Coleridge, 1785–1800*, Oxford, Clarendon Press, 2000.

Jones, F.L. (ed.), *The Letters of Percy Bysshe Shelley*, 2 vols, Oxford, Clarendon Press, 1964.

Lavater, J.C., *Essays on Physiogomy*, trans. T. Holcroft, London, G.G.J. and J. Robinson, 1793.

Massey, I., *Posthumous Poems of Shelley: Mary Shelley's Fair Copy Book*, Montreal, McGill-Queens University Press, 1969.

Medwin, T., *Conversations of Lord Byron*, ed. E.J. Lovell Jr, Princeton, NJ, Princeton University Press, 1966.

Reiman, D. et al., *Shelley and his Circle*, 10 vols to date, Cambridge, MA, Harvard University Press, 1961–.

Robinson, C. (ed.), *The Frankenstein Notebooks*, 2 vols, New York, Garland Publishing, 1996.

Robinson, C. (ed.), *The Original Frankenstein*, Oxford, Bodleian Library, 2008.

Rossetti, W.M. (ed.), *The Diary of Dr John William Polidori, 1816, Relating to Byron, Shelley, etc.* London, Elkin Matthews, 1911.

Sadler, T. (ed.), *Diary, Reminiscences and Correspondence of Henry Crabb Robinson*, 3 vols, London, Macmillan and Co., 1869.

Scott, W., review of *Frankenstein*, *Blackwood's Edinburgh Magazine*, 2 March 1818, pp. 613-20.

Shelley, M., *Frankenstein; or The Modern Prometheus* (1818), ed. M. Butler, Oxford, Oxford University Press, 1993.

Shelley, M., *Frankenstein; or The Modern Prometheus* (1831), ed. M.K. Joseph, Oxford, Oxford University Press, 1969.

Shelley, P., *Poetry and Prose*, ed. D. Reiman and Neil Fraistat, New York, W.W. Norton and Company, 2002.

Stocking, M.K. (ed.), *The Clairmont Correspondence*, 2 vols, Baltimore, MD, Johns Hopkins University Press, 1995.

Wordsworth, W., *The Major Works*, ed. S. Gill, Oxford, Oxford University Press, 1984.

SECONDARY SOURCES

Barker-Benfield, B.C., *Shelley's Guitar: an Exhibition of Manuscripts, First Editions and Relics to Mark the Bicentenary of the Birth of Percy Bysshe Shelley, 1792–1992*, Oxford, Bodleian Library, 1992.

Bennett, B.T., 'Finding Mary Shelley in Her Letters', in *Romantic Revisions*, ed. R. Brinkley and K. Hanley, Cambridge, Cambridge University Press, 1992, pp. 291–306.

Fisch, A. et al. (eds), *The Other Mary Shelley: Beyond Frankenstein*, Oxford, Oxford University Press, 1993.

Hay, D., *Young Romantics: The Shelleys, Byron and Other Tangled Lives*, London, Bloomsbury Publishing, 2010.

Hebron, S. and E. Denlinger (eds), *Shelley's Ghost: Reshaping the Image of a Literary Family*, Oxford, Bodleian Library, 2010.

Holmes, R., *Shelley: The Pursuit*, London, Harper Collins, 1974.

Mellor, A.K., *Mary Shelley: Her Life, Her Fiction, Her Monsters*, London, Routledge, 1988.

St Clair, W., *The Godwins and the Shelleys*, London, Faber and Faber, 1989.

Seymour, M., *Mary Shelley*, London, John Murray, 2000.

Todd, J., *Death and the Maidens: Fanny Wollstonecraft and the Shelley Circle*, London, Profile Books, 2007.

PICTURE CREDITS

1   Oxford, Bodleian Library, Shelley relics 39
2   © National Portrait Gallery, London
3   © National Portrait Gallery, London
4   © National Portrait Gallery, London
5   From *The Blue Poetry Book* by Andrew Lang; illustrations by H.J. Ford and L. Speed, 1891. Oxford, Bodleian Library, Walpole d.50, p. 323
6   National Gallery of Art, Washington D.C., Rosenwald Collection
7   Detroit Institute of Arts, USA/Founders Society Purchase with funds from Mr. and Mrs. Bert L. Smokler and Mr. and Mrs. Lawrence A. Fleischman/Bridgeman Images
8   Bibliothèque nationale de France, Paris
9   British Museum/Bridgeman Images
10 Oxford, Bodleian Library, 3 Delta 1179, Tom VII pag. 418
11 National Gallery of Art, Washington DC, Rosenwald Collection, 1944.5.39
12 Image courtesy of Rare Books and Special Collections, The University of Sydney Library
13 Princeton, Historic Maps Collection
14 © National Portrait Gallery, London
15 Oxford, Bodleian Library, MS. Abinger e. 8, fol. 26v
16 © National Portrait Gallery, London
17 Oxford, Bodleian Library, Shelley relics (d)
18 Courtesy of Newstead Abbey, Nottingham City Museums and Galleries
19 Oxford, Bodleian Library, MS. Abinger d. 27, fol. 52v
20 Private Collection

21 Oxford, Bodleian Library, (OC) 250 a.317
22 Victoria and Albert Museum
23 Carl H. Pforzheimer Collection, New York Public Library
24 Oxford, Bodleian Library, MS. Abinger c. 66, fol. 18r
25 Carl H. Pforzheimer Collection, New York Public Library
26 © Tate, London 2017
27 Oxford, Bodleian Library, MS. Shelley adds. c. 4, fol. 71v
28 Oxford, Bodleian Library, MS. Shelley adds. e. 18, p. 106 rev
29 Yale Centre for British Art, Paul Mellon Collection
30 Oxford, Bodleian Library, MS. Shelley adds. e. 16, p. 13
31 Oxford, Bodleian Library, MS. Eng. misc. c. 198, fol. 125r
32 Oxford, Bodleian Library, Shelley relics 40 / Nick Cistone
33 British Library, London, UK/© British Library Board. All Rights Reserved/ Bridgeman Images
34 Hamburger Kunsthalle/ Bridgeman Images
35 Oxford, Bodleian Library, MS. Abinger c. 56, fol. 4r
36 Oxford, Bodleian Library, MS. Abinger c. 57, fol. 94v
37 Oxford, Bodleian Library, MS. Abinger c. 57, fore-edge and head (before mounting)
38 Oxford, Bodleian Library, MS. Abinger c. 56, fol. 3r
39 Oxford, Bodleian Library, MS. Abinger c. 57, fol. 22r

40   Oxford, Bodleian Library, MS Abinger
      c. 56, fols 11v–12r
41   Oxford, Bodleian Library, MS Abinger
      c. 56, fol. 12v
42   Oxford, Bodleian Library, Shelley adds.
      d. 6, p. 24
43   Oxford, Bodleian Library, Arch. AA
      e.167(v.1)
44   Oxford, Bodleian Library, Shelley
      relics 36
45   Oxford, Bodleian Library, Buxton 201
46   Oxford, Bodleian Library, N. 2706 d.10,
      p. 235
47   Wikimedia/Creative Commons
48   © Geraint Lewis/Alamy
49   Oxford, Bodleian Library, John Johnson
      Collection
50   National Museums of Liverpool, Walker
      Art Gallery/Bridgeman Images
51   Oxford, Bodleian Library, MS. Abinger
      d. 30, fol. 1r
52   Oxford, Bodleian Library, Shelley
      relics (g)
53   Oxford, Bodleian Library, 2795 f.38
54   Oxford, Bodleian Library, MS. Photogr.
      c. 185, fol. 75
55   © Helen Drinkwater

INDEX